Recetas de Viejo Mexico
Recipes of Old Mexico

Compiled by Carol Blakely
Edited by Jeanne Wright and Arturo Medina

Penfield
BOOKS

SO-AUP-691

A Rich Heritage

Before the Spaniard Hernando Cortés conquered Mexico in 1519-1521, four unique civilizations flourished there: the Mayas, the Olmecs, the Toltecs, and the Aztecs. Spain ruled Mexico for 300 years until the Mexican revolt in 1810 brought independence in 1821. Mexico is a federal republic of over 108 million people primarily of Amerindian and Spanish descent. Mexico is bordered by the United States, the Gulf of Mexico, Pacific Ocean, Guatemala and Belize. Climate varies from tropical to desert.

The front cover illustration and others on pages 3 and 172 show details from Mayan picture writing from a 14th-century Mayan manuscript. Now in the British Museum, this collection was first published by the Peabody Institute in The Codex Nuttall, A Picture Manuscript from Ancient Mexico, *edited by Zelia Nuttal, reprinted by Dover Publications.*

ISBN 1-932043-43-8 © *2007 Penfield Books*

Contents

Associate editors: Miriam Canter, Dorothy Crum, Melinda Bradnan, Jacque Gharib, Hope Solomons, and Joan Liffring-Zug Bourret

Antojitos – Appetizers

Mexico has a long tradition of serving appetizers before meals. The word *antojitos* is the Spanish term for "little whims," and they were originally small treats made of *masa* dough or tortillas. This term is now used to refer to all appetizers, although most are eaten with tortillas.

Mexican Good Luck Omens

To see or hear a sparrow hawk announces unexpected wealth.
If you see a rabbit on your way to market, you will sell all your goods.

Nuez de Saltillo – Saltillo Nuts

1/4 cup butter
2 cups pecan halves
1 tablespoon soy sauce

1 teaspoon salt
1 tablespoon chili powder
4 or 5 dashes Tabasco™ Sauce

Melt butter in shallow pan and spread pecans evenly in one layer. Bake at 325° for 30 minutes or until nuts begin to brown, stirring once or twice while baking. Mix soy sauce, salt, chili powder, and Tabasco™ Sauce and stir into the toasted nuts, mixing well. Spread on paper towels to cool. Store in air tight container. Makes 2 cups.

Chile con Queso – Cheese and Chile Dip

2 tablespoons oil
1 onion, chopped
2 cloves garlic, minced
2 large ripe tomatoes,
   peeled and chopped

1 (4-ounce) can chopped
   green chiles
2-1/2 cups grated Longhorn
   Cheddar cheese
Salt and pepper to taste

Heat oil in skillet, add onion, and cook until limp, add garlic and cook 1 minute more. Add tomatoes, green chiles, cheese, salt, and pepper. Cook on low until cheese melts. Serve with corn tortilla chips.

Tostadas – Crisp Corn Tortillas

Tostadas are whole corn tortillas, fried crisp. You can purchase bags of tostadas in the Mexican food section of your grocery store. They are also easy to make; simply fry tortillas in hot oil until crisp. For a low fat version, the tortillas can also be baked in the oven until crisp. Tostadas can be topped with fillings as simple as grated cheese or more elaborate fillings like the spinach and bacon filling described on page 10.

A Mexican Salute

Salud, amor, pesetas, y tiempo para gozarlas
Health, love, wealth, and the time to enjoy them

Quesadillas Mexicanas – Mexican Turnovers

Quesadillas are easy to make and can be as simple as a sliver of cheese folded inside a tortilla and cooked on the griddle until the cheese is melted.

2 cold baked potatoes, peeled, chopped
1/2 small onion, chopped
2 cloves garlic, minced
1 (4-ounce) can green chiles
12 corn tortillas
Oil for frying

1 tomato, chopped
2 tablespoons chopped onion
2 jalapeño chiles, chopped
1/4 head lettuce, shredded
Sour cream

Cook potatoes, onion, and garlic in 2 tablespoons of oil until potatoes are browned. Add green chiles and cook 3 or 4 minutes more. Soften corn tortillas and fill with potato mixture. Fold in half and fry in 1/4-inch hot oil until crisp. To soften tortillas, spray lightly with non-stick cooking spray, wrap in paper towels, and cook on high in microwave for 60 seconds. (See page 18 for methods of softening tortillas.) Chop tomato, onion, and jalapeños together until very fine, season to taste with salt. Open each fried quesadilla and add some of the tomato mixture, lettuce, and sour cream.

Festival del Gourmet

Puerto Vallarta, Jalisco, attracts 20,000 people annually to its November food festival. Local chefs and guest chefs from around the world serve gourmet foods, cheese, tequilas, and liquors. Cooking classes, wine tasting, and beer samples are are offered. Another festival of Gastronómico *is held in Cancun, Quintana Roo.*

Tostadas de Espinaca – Spinach and Bacon Tostadas

1 tablespoon oil
1 chopped onion
2 cloves garlic, minced
1/4 teaspoon salt

1 teaspoon chili powder
1 package frozen spinach, cooked
    and thoroughly drained
Juice of 1/2 lime

6 to 8 corn tortillas, fried crisp or store-bought tostadas
6 pieces of bacon, fried crisp and crumbled
1 to 1-1/2 cups shredded Queso Blanco or Monterey Jack cheese

Heat oil in skillet, add onion and garlic, and sauté. Add salt and chili powder to mix, then add spinach and lime juice and cook until all liquid is cooked away. Spread spinach mixture on tostada, sprinkle with crumbled bacon and cheese. Place tostadas on cookie sheet and bake in 450° oven until cheese bubbles. Serve immediately with salsa.

Picadillo – Mexican Meat Hash

1 pound ground beef
1 pound ground pork
1 onion, chopped
4 cloves garlic, minced
4 tomatoes, peeled and
    chopped

1/2 cup tomato paste
1 cup raisins
1/2 cup chopped almonds
2 pickled jalapeños, chopped
1 cup water
Salt to taste

Brown meat in heavy skillet; drain off excess fat. Add onion, garlic, and tomatoes to meat and cook until onion is limp. Add other ingredients and simmer on low for 30 to 40 minutes. Serve with chips or tortillas. This filling can also be used as filling for empanadas (meat turnovers) and for tacos.

Nachos – Tortilla Chip Snack

6 corn tortillas
1/2 cup refried beans

1/2 cup grated Cheddar or
Longhorn cheese
1/3 cup pickled jalapeño pepper
slices

Cut tortillas into quarters. Fry in hot oil until crisp; drain on paper towels. Spread refried beans on quarters, sprinkle with cheese and top with 2 or 3 jalapeño slices. Broil until cheese melts. Serve immediately.

Mexican Saying
El que de suerte vive, de suerte muere.
He who rises by luck, falls by luck, too.

Queso Relleno – Stuffed Edam Cheese

Edam cheeses were first imported into the seaports of the state of Yucatán. This recipe, which originated in Yucatán, makes a great appetizer.

1 (1-pound) round Edam cheese
1/2 pound ground pork
1/2 onion, chopped
2 garlic cloves, minced

2 ripe tomatoes, peeled and chopped
1 (4-ounce) can sliced black olives
Salt and pepper to taste

Sauce:
2 tablespoons oil
2 tablespoons chopped onion
1 (4-ounce) can chopped green chiles

2 ripe tomatoes, peeled and chopped
2 jalapeño peppers, finely chopped

(continued)

Using a potato peeler, peel red wax skin from cheese. Cut a thin slice from top and, using a spoon, carefully hollow out the cheese ball, leaving a 1/2-inch shell. Reserve the scooped out cheese for other uses. Soak cheese shell in lukewarm water for 1 hour.

Cook ground pork, onion, and garlic in skillet until meat is cooked through. Stir in other ingredients and simmer on low for about 5 minutes.

Drain cheese shell and pat dry. Brush outside with oil. Place cheese shell in close-fitting baking dish. Spoon the pork mixture into the cheese shell. Bake uncovered in 350° oven for 12 to 15 minutes or until cheese shell begins to melt. For sauce, heat oil and add onion and green chiles. Add ripe tomatoes and jalapeño peppers. Cook on low for about 10 minutes. Pour over melted cheese ball. Serve immediately with warm tortillas.

Tortas – Bean Sandwiches

4 *bolillos* – Mexican rolls	1/2 cup salsa
1 cup refried beans	Lettuce
1/2 cup grated cheese	Chopped tomato

Split *bolillos* in half lengthwise and scoop out some of the bread. Spread about 1/4 cup of the refried beans on one half of the roll. Add 2 tablespoons grated cheese, 2 tablespoons salsa, and top with lettuce and tomato. Place other half of *bolillos* on top to make sandwich. Makes 4 sandwiches.

Mantequilla de Pobre – " Butter of the Poor " – Avocado Dip

Avocados are rich in oil and, when ripe, the green meat of the avocado can be spread on bread just like butter.

4 avocados, peeled, coarsely mashed
4 tomatoes, finely sliced
2 bunches green onions, sliced
1-1/2 teaspoon salt
2 tablespoons chopped fresh cilantro

2 tablespoons olive oil
1/4 cup lime or lemon juice
1 (4-ounce) can chopped green
    chiles

Mix avocados, tomatoes, and onions. Add other ingredients. Let stand in refrigerator 30 minutes before serving. Use as a dip with corn tortilla chips.

Masa y Tortillas – Corn and Tortillas

Corn originated from a small grass native to the Sierra Madre area of western Mexico. Six thousand years before Columbus reached the Americas, the plant had evolved into a major food crop throughout both American continents. Corn was the most important food source in pre-Hispanic times. Tortillas were the primary bread of Mexican natives as far back as 4000 B.C. Aztec and Mayan creation myths are based on corn legends.

The Mayan creation myth tells how the gods created people from *masa* (corn flour dough). The yellow of the corn was considered to be part of the sun's rays, and growing corn in the field was a daily tribute to the corn god.

How to Soften Tortillas

Traditional Method
Place a little oil in skillet and heat until very hot. Using tongs, take each tortilla and dip in hot oil, turning so both sides are coated. This should take a few seconds for each tortilla. Some recipes call for then dipping the tortillas in enchilada sauce. You would then repeat the step above, except this time you would have sauce in the skillet rather than oil.

Microwave Method
Spray each tortilla on both sides with non-stick cooking spray. Wrap a stack of tortillas in a paper towel and place in microwave and cook on high for 60 seconds. You will have perfectly soft tortillas without the oil of the traditional method.

Combine the Methods
When recipes call for first softening the tortillas, then dipping in a sauce, use the microwave method for the first step, then dip the tortillas in the cooked sauce on the stove for the second step.

Tortillas de Masa – Corn Tortillas

This recipe calls for masa harina *(corn flour), which is sold in the Mexican food section of most grocery stores.*

2 cups *masa harina*	2 tablespoons butter
1 teaspoon salt	1-1/4 cups warm water

Mix *masa harina* and salt together. Add butter. Make a hole in center of flour and add water. Work into a soft dough. Knead until no longer sticky. Let rest for 20 minutes. Form dough into 12 to 16 balls. If you use a tortilla press, line the press with a piece of waxed paper or a plastic sandwich bag, place ball in press, cover with more waxed paper or plastic bag, and close the press to flatten the ball. Remove and peel off paper or plastic.

(continued)

If made by hand, pat ball in hands, moving in a circular motion until a thin pancake about 6 inches in diameter is formed. Place on hot griddle and cook a few seconds until edges begin to dry, flip over and cook on other side until it is lightly browned, then flip again to finish cooking the first side. Allow about 2 minutes for each side.

Five Lost Days of the Mayan Calendar

The Mayan year was divided into 18 months of 20 days each. This left five unlucky days without names at the end of the year. The Spanish chroniclers wrote that no action of any importance, even sweeping the house or combing one's hair, was to be undertaken. Woe to the poor person who happened to be born during one of the nameless days. His life was fated to be one of misery and unhappiness.

Tortillas de Harina – Wheat Flour Tortillas

The Spanish introduced wheat to Mexico. Flour tortillas are popular in the northern wheat growing regions of Mexico. If you have never tasted a thick, soft, freshly-made flour tortilla, you are missing a treat.

3 cups flour
3 teaspoons baking powder
1 teaspoon salt

3 tablespoons oil (use more for
   softer tortillas)
1 cup water

Mix together flour, baking powder, and salt. Make a hole in the center and pour in oil and water. Mix well to form a soft dough. Knead dough 15 to 20 times and allow to rest for 20 minutes. Divide into 10 balls. Place ball on lightly floured board and roll out to a thickness of about 1/2 inch. Tortillas can also be formed using a tortilla press. Cook on a very hot ungreased griddle until lightly browned on both sides.

Enchiladas Básicas – Basic Enchiladas

One of the most famous Mexican dishes made from tortillas is enchiladas, which means "in chile." All types of food can be folded, rolled, or stuffed into corn tortillas, which are then covered in a chile sauce. Cheese enchiladas are easy to make and are the most popular fare served in Mexican restaurants in the United States.

12 corn tortillas
4 cups red chile sauce
   (canned or homemade)

3 cups grated Cheddar cheese
1 onion, chopped fine
Ripe black olives, optional

Prepare corn tortillas as described on page 18, first softening, then cooking in a little red chile sauce. Place about 3 tablespoons of grated cheese on tortilla, and sprinkle a little onion on top and roll up tightly. Grease shallow baking dish and spoon a little of the chile sauce in the bottom, then starting at the end, place enchiladas, open side down in the baking dish. Continue making enchiladas and placing in row in baking dish. When all are finished, pour remaining chile sauce over the enchiladas. Top with remaining cheese, optional ripe black olive slices can be sprinkled on top of the cheese. Bake in 400° oven for 25 minutes or until sauce is bubbling and cheese has melted. Makes 6 to 8 servings. This dish can be made a day ahead and stored in refrigerator until time to bake.

Variations: A ground meat mixture such as *picadillo* can be used in place of the cheese. Chicken, pork, or scrambled eggs can also be used for the filling. Substitute green chile sauce for the red chile sauce.

More enchilada recipes follow and the variations are endless.

Enchiladas de Espinaca – Sour Cream Spinach Enchiladas

Jalapeño peppers go well with spinach and add zest to this vegetarian recipe.

1 package frozen chopped spinach,
    cooked and well drained
1 tablespoon salad oil
1/2 cup chopped onion
2 cloves garlic, chopped
1 tablespoon finely chopped pickled
    jalapeño
2 tablespoons juice from pickled
    jalapeño or 2 tablespoons cider vinegar
8 ounces Monterey Jack cheese, grated (divided)

1 (4-ounce) can chopped green
    chiles (divided)
1/2 teaspoon salt
2 tablespoons butter
2 tablespoons flour
1-1/4 cups milk
1 cup sour cream
8 to 10 corn tortillas

Spinach Filling:

Drain all liquid from cooked spinach. Heat oil in small skillet and add onions. Cook until limp, add minced garlic and cook 1 or 2 minutes more. Add chopped jalapeños, jalapeño pickle juice or vinegar, 1/2 can of chopped green chiles, and cook until all liquid is absorbed; 3 to 5 minutes. Add 1/2 teaspoon salt or enough to correct the taste. Set mixture aside.

Sour Cream Sauce:

Melt butter in skillet, add flour and stir until smooth, taking care to keep from burning. Add milk and stir or whisk until sauce has thickened. Turn off heat before adding sour cream to prevent curdling. Add sour cream, 1/2 of the grated cheese, and remaining 1/2 can of green chiles, stirring to mix. Add salt to taste.   *(continued)*

Soften corn tortillas according to methods described on page 18.

To assemble enchiladas:

Spray rectangular baking dish with non-stick cooking spray. Spoon a little of the sour cream sauce in dish to barely cover bottom. To make the enchiladas, spoon 2 to 3 tablespoons of the spinach filling onto the tortilla and roll up. Lay open side down in the baking dish on top of the sour cream sauce. Continue until all the tortillas are filled and placed in the dish. Pour remaining sour cream sauce over the enchiladas.

Sprinkle remaining Monterey Jack cheese on top. Bake in 425° oven for 12 to 15 minutes until the cheese is melted and enchiladas are heated through.

Enchiladas de Langosta – Green Lobster Enchiladas

Salsa verde *(green sauce)* is sold in the Mexican food section of most grocery stores.

1 tablespoon oil
1/2 onion, finely chopped
2 (6-ounce) cans *salsa verde**
2 tablespoons chopped cilantro
1 teaspoon salt

1/2 cup cream or evaporated milk
2 cups cooked lobster meat
2 tablespoons lemon juice
1 cup grated Monterey Jack cheese
12 corn tortillas (see page 18)

Heat oil in heavy skillet, add onions; sauté until soft. Add *salsa verde*, cilantro,

*See page 44

(continued)

salt, and cream. Simmer on low for 5 minutes. Set aside.

Dip softened tortillas in green sauce, fill with equal parts of lobster, sprinkle with lemon juice, and a spoon of the green sauce. Roll up and place open side down in rectangular baking dish. Pour remaining sauce over enchiladas; top with cheese. Bake in 425° oven for 15 minutes until heated through. Serve with sour cream.

Mayan Creation Myth

The Mayan gods created people to keep them company. The first people were made of mud and melted in the rain. The next people were made of wood and were stiff with no emotions. Then the gods created people made of corn dough (masa) *who had feelings and emotions and who praised the gods who had created them.*

Enchiladas Suizas – Swiss Enchiladas

The Mexicans have a custom of calling recipes containing cream "Swiss" dishes.

2 cups diced cooked chicken
2 (4-ounce) cans diced green chiles
8 ounces shredded Monterey Jack cheese, (divided)
8 to 10 corn tortillas
1 pint heavy cream

Combine the chicken, green chiles, and half of the cheese.

Soften corn tortillas according to suggestions. Heat cream on low heat and dip each tortilla in the cream. Place about 1/4 cup of the filling in each corn tortilla and roll up. Place in large greased baking dish, open side down. Continue until all the tortillas are filled and placed in the baking dish. Pour remaining cream over the tortillas and sprinkle remaining cheese on top. Bake at 425° for about 30 minutes until golden brown and cheese melted. Serve with sliced tomatoes and guacamole.

Tacos – Snacks

Another favorite food made from the corn tortilla is the taco. In the U. S., people are used to crisp tortillas, but the Mexicans like their tacos lightly fried and still a little chewy. Another variation is the soft taco, where the tortilla is warmed and softened, but not fried or cooked any further. Tacos can be filled with a ground beef mixture, such as picadillo, *cooked chicken, shredded pork, such as* carnitas, *fried potatoes, and grated cheese. The fillings are left up to your imagination and foods you have on hand.*

To make your own tacos in the Mexican style, soften the corn tortillas as described on page 18. In the center of each tortilla, place about 1/4 cup filling. Fold tortilla in half and fry in hot oil about 1/4-inch deep. Let become almost crisp on one side, turn and cook other side. Drain on paper towels. Stuff with lettuce and tomatoes, salsa, and/or sour cream.

Green Pork Tacos made with soft tortillas: Soften tortillas as described. Spoon about 1/4 cup pork *carnitas* and 1 tablespoon of a mixture of 1/2 cup fresh chopped cilantro and chopped onion. Top with green sauce and sour cream. Fold in half and eat.

Filling suggestions:
Ground beef *picadillo* filling. Add a garnish of shredded lettuce with tomato, top with grated cheese and salsa.

Cooked chicken mixed with green chiles, topped with lettuce and avocado slices.

Cooked pork, topped with chopped cilantro and chopped onion, *salsa verde*, and sour cream.

(continued)

Soft fried potatoes with grated cheese and onion, topped with salsa.

Chopped roast beef with chopped onion and red chile sauce. Topped with lettuce, tomato, and sour cream.

Voladores de Papantla – The Dance of the *Voladores*

Totonac Indians, the flying men of Veracruz, perform an ancient ritual, dating back thousands of years, for the celebration of the harvesting of vanilla beans. The men are up 60 to 100 feet on a large pole with a revolving platform. Music of a flute and drum sound and prayers are chanted initally to Xipe Totec, God of Fertility, for rains to return. The roped men spiral head down and outward toward the ground as ropes unwind.

Chilaquiles – Tortilla Hash

This recipe is usually prepared with left-over tortillas. Cooked chicken or beef can be added to the dish.

12 corn tortillas
Oil for frying
2 onions, chopped
3 cloves garlic, minced
2 tablespoons oil
1/2 cup chopped bell pepper

2 (8-ounce) cans tomato sauce
1 teaspoon salt
2 to 3 tablespoons red chili powder
1 cup grated cheese
1 (4-ounce) can sliced ripe olives, drained

(continued)

Cut tortillas into 1-inch squares. Fry in oil until light brown, but not crisp. Drain on paper towels. Sauté the onion, garlic, and bell pepper in the 2 tablespoons oil. Add tomato sauce, salt, and chili powder, and simmer for 20 minutes, stirring occasionally to keep from burning. Add tortilla pieces and cook for 5 minutes more. Pour mixture into 2-quart casserole and sprinkle with the cheese. Top with the ripe olives. Bake in 350° oven for 20 minutes or until cheese has melted.

Día de los Muertos – Day of the Dead

This national holiday dates back to pre-Hispanic times. The Spanish attempted to remove the pagan tones of the celebration by changing the date from midsummer to All Saint's Day in November. Now, as then, families gather at grave sites, sharing food and drink with the departed. Burial grounds are decorated with colorful flowers, papers, and candles. The skull (calavera) symbolizes this day.

Tamales

Tamales are an ancient dish. Bernal Díaz Del Castillo describes many varieties of tamales being sold at the markets in 1519. The most popular filling for tamales is pork, but beef or chicken can be used. Sweet tamales containing sugar and candied fruits are made at Christmas as a treat for the children. Making tamales is a time-consuming task. It is easier to prepare the meat a day before making the tamales. Tamales freeze well.

2 to 3 pounds lean pork
1 onion, quartered
2 cloves garlic

1 cup red chile sauce or 1/4 cup
   chili powder
1 cup meat stock

Place meat in heavy pan with onion and garlic, cover with water and simmer

(continued)

until meat is tender, about 2 to 3 hours. Allow meat to cool in broth. Remove meat and shred, adding the red chile sauce or chili powder and meat stock. Add salt and pepper to taste. If meat is dry, add more stock.

Tamal Dough:

5 to 6 dozen corn husks, trimmed and washed	3-1/2 cups warm water
	2 cups shortening or lard
6 cups *masa harina*	2 teaspoons salt

Place the corn husks in warm water to soak until soft. Mix *masa harina* and warm water to make a thick dough. In a large bowl, beat the shortening or lard with the salt until fluffy. Add the *masa* dough to the creamed shortening, mixing well. To form the *tamal*, spread about 2 tablespoons of the *masa* dough on the corn husk, making a rectangle about 4x3 inches and leaving a margin around the edges. Place about 2 tablespoons of the meat mixture down the center of the *masa* dough. Fold the lengthwise edge, making sure the *masa* is covering the meat. Fold the top and bottom edges of the corn husk down. Lay the *tamal*, folded side down, into a steamer basket that has been lined with corn husks. Continue making tamales and placing open side down in the steamer. Heat water to boiling in steamer, fit steamer basket on top, cover and steam for 45 to 50 minutes or until the tamales are cooked through. When the *tamal* is done, it will be easy to unwrap with no dough sticking to the corn husk. Watch water level and add boiling water to steamer as needed. The tamales should be stacked only two or three deep, so it may be necessary to steam them in two batches. Makes 5 to 6 dozen tamales.

Gorditas – Little Fat Ones

These little masa *cakes can be made ahead, then stuffed right before serving with* picadillo, carnitas, *or scrambled eggs and sausage.*

2 cups *masa harina*
1 teaspoon baking powder
1 teaspoon salt

1 cup water
Oil for frying

Mix the ingredients to form a stiff dough. Pinch off small portions of dough and form 2-inch balls. Flatten to form a patty about 3 inches wide and 1/2-inch thick. Fry in hot oil until golden brown, turn to cook on both sides. Drain on paper towels. Make a slit through the middle, open slightly and stuff in meat or egg filling. Top with shredded lettuce, tomatoes, and grated cheese. Serve with salsa. Makes 8 *gorditas*.

Salsas – Sauces

What would Mexican cuisine be without its chile salsas? Each meal is accompanied by at least one table sauce, sometimes with cooked ingredients and sometimes raw ingredients. In Mexico, chile pepper cultivation goes back thousands of years. Open markets sell the peppers just as the Aztecs and Mayans did in bright stacks of orange, red, green, and yellow. Columbus carried the first chile pepper plants to Europe in 1493. Easy to grow, cultivation of chiles spread to all of Europe, India, China and Japan. Chile peppers, rich in vitamins and prized for medicinal qualities, replaced the more expensive black pepper as a flavoring. Many recipes, including enchiladas or chilaquiles, call for chile sauce as an ingredient. Recipes in this book are for basic cooked sauces and fresh table salsas plus a few more exotic recipes. The next page lists popular peppers used.

Popular Peppers

Ancho—dried, 4 to 5 inches, deep red, medium hot, for cooked salsas

Poblano—fresh, 4 to 5 inches dark green, medium hot, for stuffing/flavoring

Serrano—fresh, 1 to 2 inches, green, very hot, for sauces and flavoring

Jalapeño—fresh, 2 to 3 inches, green or red, very hot, for salsas/stuffing, flavor

Habanero—fresh, 1 inch round, orange, fiery hot, for salsas, flavoring

Guajillo—dried, 2 to 3 inches, dark red, hot, for cooked salsas

Chipotle—dried and smoked, sometimes canned in adobo sauce, dark red, very hot, smoky flavor used for seasoning

New Mexico Red—4 to 5 inches, deep red, mild, for cooked sauces

Chile de Arbol—2 inches, red, very hot, for flavoring, use sparingly

Chile Japonés—small, 1/8 inch, red, very hot, flavoring, use sparingly

Anaheim or California—fresh, 4 inch, dark green, mild, sauces and flavoring

Salsa Brava – Brave Sauce

This is an authentic Mexican recipe for chile sauce. If you can't find the types of chiles listed, try substituting other dried chiles.

20 *cascabel* chiles
10 *guajillo* chiles
5 *Chiles de Arboles*
1 cinnamon stick (very small)
10 whole peppercorns

Dash of cumin
1 teaspoon ground oregano
3 teaspoons vinegar
1 whole onion
4 garlic cloves

Wash and boil the chiles for 20 minutes. Let soak for another 20 minutes. Blend with all other ingredients. Add salt to taste. Mixture thickens as it cools. Relish keeps for several weeks in refrigerator.

Salsa Colorada – Red Chile Sauce

This is the most basic red chile sauce that can be used for making enchiladas and other dishes. It can be used to season soups and served as a table sauce.

10 to 12 New Mexico dried red
    chile peppers
Boiling water
2 cloves garlic
1/2 teaspoon Mexican oregano

3 tablespoons oil
3 tablespoons flour
3 tablespoons rice wine vinegar
2 teaspoons salt
Water

Stem, seed, and de-vein the peppers. Place each pepper on hot dry skillet for a few seconds to toast. Rinse peppers and place in a glass bowl. Pour boiling water over the peppers to cover. Let soak for 1/2 hour.

Place peppers, garlic, and oregano in food processor and process until smooth. Add some of the soaking water and process again. Process about 5 minutes until very smooth and creamy with the consistency of thin cream. Put the mixture through a strainer to remove small particles of dried chile skin.

Heat the oil in a heavy skillet. Add the flour and cook until light brown. Add the chile mixture, rice wine vinegar, and salt, and cook over medium-low heat for 15 minutes. Stir constantly to keep from burning. Taste and correct the seasoning by adding more salt or wine vinegar. Add water to thin as needed. The sauce should have a consistency of thin gravy. Makes 5 to 6 cups. This makes enough to use in two enchilada recipes. The unused sauce can be frozen. You can also make this sauce with *ancho* chiles. The *ancho* chile is the ripe dried version of the *poblano*. The *poblano* is not as hot as jalapeños.

Salsa Verde – Green Sauce

1 pound fresh *tomatillos*
2 fresh green chile peppers,
  poblano or California
1/2 onion, chopped

1/4 cup chopped cilantro
1 teaspoon salt
1/2 cup chicken broth

Remove husks from *tomatillos*, rinse and place in saucepan with water to cover. Cook on medium high until tender. Drain and chop *tomatillos*.

Place *tomatillos* and remaining ingredients in blender or food processor. Process until smooth. Pour purée into saucepan, bring to boil, lower heat, and simmer about 10 minutes.

Use this sauce for green enchiladas or as a table sauce.

Salsa Fresca – Fresh Sauce

Red ripe tomatoes are a must for this sauce. When you buy Roma tomatoes, do not refrigerate, but leave out on the counter or window sill, and they will continue to ripen.

4 ripe Roma tomatoes
3 *serrano* chiles, minced
1 clove garlic
1/2 small onion, chopped

1 tablespoon oil
1/2 teaspoon salt
1 tablespoon cider vinegar or
    freshly-squeezed lime juice

Plunge tomatoes into boiling water to loosen skin. Remove from hot water and run cold water over tomatoes to cool. Core tomatoes and remove skins,

(continued)

then roughly dice. For less heat, remove seeds from the *serranos* before mincing. Put all ingredients in food processor or blender and process briefly. Let stand in refrigerator 1/2 hour before serving. Makes 1-1/2 cups. You can substitute fresh jalapeño peppers for the *serrano* chiles.

World Heritage Sites

Many of the sites were ancient ceremonial centers of the Teotihuacans, Zapotecos, Totonacas, and Mayans. Important archaeological sites are: Teotihuacán in the state of Mexico; Monte Albán in Oaxaca; El Tajín in Veracruz; Uxmal and Chichen Itzá on the Yucatán Peninsula. Courtyards, temples and pyramids are in Mexico City, Puebla, Oaxaca, Campeche, Zacatecas, Querétaro, Guanajuato, and Morelia.

Salsa de Piña – Pineapple Sauce

Pineapple is thought to be a native plant of Brazil; it is popular in Mexico. Try to find ripe, firm pineapple when making this salsa. Serve with fish or chicken.

2 cups fresh pineapple, cut into
    small chunks
1/2 cup chopped red bell pepper
1/2 medium onion, chopped
3 or 4 fresh jalapeño peppers, chopped

2 tablespoons rice wine vinegar
1 teaspoon sugar
1/2 teaspoon salt

Place pineapple, bell pepper, onion, and jalapeños in bowl. Combine vinegar, sugar, and salt, stirring until sugar and salt are dissolved. Pour over pineapple mixture, stir to coat all pieces. Refrigerate 30 minutes before serving.

Jalapeño Relish

1 pound fresh jalapeño peppers	2-1/2 cups apple cider vinegar
1 large onion, chopped	3-1/2 cups sugar
4 to 5 large carrots	1 tablespoon mustard seed
1 large red bell pepper, stems and seeds removed	1 tablespoon dill seed
	1 teaspoon salt

Wearing rubber gloves to protect hands, slice jalapeños in half, removing stems, seeds, and membranes; cut into julienne strips. Clean and julienne onion, carrots, and red bell pepper. Combine sugar and vinegar in large saucepan over medium heat. Stir until sugar dissolves. Add all vegetables and bring to a boil. Lower heat; simmer for 20 to 25 minutes until mixture begins to thicken.

Add spices and salt; continue simmering for another 30 to 35 minutes. Remove from heat. Mixture will thicken as it cools. Relish keeps for several weeks in refrigerator.

Note: Jalapeño is the most popular of the green chile peppers. These 2 to 3-inch long peppers are hot. Jalapeños in the green or unripe stage are sold fresh, canned, and pickled.

Editor Arturo Medina adds: *While in the United States, the jalapeño pepper is the most popular, in Mexico the* serrano *pepper is more commonly used.*

Salsa de Crema y Jalapeño – Creamy Jalapeño Sauce

A little known fact is that cream goes well with chiles. Here is an example of a creamy jalapeño sauce. Serve this sauce with grilled meats and fish.

10 fresh jalapeño peppers   1 finely-chopped onion
1 cup heavy cream   Salt and pepper to taste

Toast the jalapeños on a grill until dark brown. Peel and dice them. Combine the jalapeños with the other ingredients.

Arturo Medina advises: *Cream and dairy products dissolve the heat of a hot pepper. This is a good home remedy for a very hot salsa or chile. Adding ice cream is the best.*

Salsa Borracha – Drunken Sauce

If you cannot find pasilla *chiles, substitute 3 or 4* ancho *chiles (anchos are larger than* pasillas.)

1/2 cup peanut oil	1/2 teaspoon salt
6 *pasilla* chiles	1 small onion, finely chopped
1 cup orange juice	1/2 cup tequila

Heat the oil and fry the chilies. Remove and drain on paper towels. Cool and remove the stems and crush a bit. Blend the chiles, juice, and salt until almost smooth. Cook the onion in a little oil until soft. Add the sauce and continue cooking over medium heat for about 5 minutes. Set aside to cool. Before serving, stir in the tequila.

Salsa de Repollo – Fresh Cabbage Sauce

This sauce makes a perfect accompaniment to fish or pork dishes.

1 small head of cabbage,
    finely shredded
Juice of 1 orange
Juice of 1 lime
1 tablespoon rice wine vinegar

2 tablespoons pickled jalapeños,
    minced
2 tablespoons olive oil
1 teaspoon sugar
1 teaspoon salt

Put shredded cabbage in salad bowl. Mix other ingredients and pour over cabbage, tossing to combine. Cover and let stand in refrigerator for 30 minutes before serving.

Pico de Gallo – Beak of the Rooster

This popular raw sauce is made two ways. Carol Blakely writes, "One is with jícama, oranges, and other fresh fruits sprinkled with chili powder. Arturo Medina adds, "The pico de gallo with tomato, onion, pepper and cilantro is known as Salsa Mexicana with the colors of green, white, and red, which signify the Mexican flag." The recipe for the latter version follows.

4 or 5 ripe plum tomatoes, chopped | 1/2 cup fresh cilantro, chopped
1/2 white onion, chopped | Juice of 1 lime
3 or 4 fresh jalapeños, chopped | 1 teaspoon salt

Mix all ingredients in small bowl. Chill for 30 minutes before serving.

Ensaladas – Salads

Mexicans have always eaten plenty of raw greens, fruits, and vegetables, mostly in the form of salsas and garnishes. When Mexicans do serve salads, they are usually *ensaladas compuestas* – composed salads, with the ingredients arranged in an eye-pleasing design on the plate.

Avocado trees were cultivated in Mexico in 8000 BC The fruit is called *Mantequilla de los Pobres* or "Butter of the Poor." In Mexico, it is common to see a bowl of fresh avocados on the dinner table; the avocados can be cut and the pulp spread on warm tortillas and bread. The avocado, while rich in oil and oleic acid, a monounsaturated fat, is one of the world's healthiest foods. Spanish historian Bernal Díaz wrote that servants of the Aztec King Montezuma, prepared guacamole at the table and served it to him with thin white tortillas.

Simple Classic Guacamole

4 ripe avocados
1 ripe plum tomato
Juice of 1 lime

2 cloves garlic, finely minced
Salt to taste

Place avocado pulp in a bowl and roughly mash, leaving some lumps for texture. Cut end off tomato and grate the pulp, discarding the skin. Mash the garlic and salt together and add to avocado mixture. Add lime juice and mix well. Let stand 15 or 20 minutes for flavor to develop. Squeeze lime juice over leftover guacamole to keep from darkening. Cover and refrigerate. Serve as a salad on a bed of shredded lettuce. Makes 6 servings.

Ensalada de Garbanzo – Chick Pea Salad

Garbanzos or chick peas were brought to Spain by Arab traders. The Spanish later introduced the garbanzo to Mexico where it was quickly assimilated into their cuisine. Garbanzos are one of the world's healthiest foods. This is an easy-to-make salad using canned beans.

1 (16-ounce) can garbanzo beans, drained
1/4 cup chopped green onion
1 (4-ounce) can chopped green chiles
1 (4-ounce) jar chopped pimientos

2 tablespoons olive oil
1/4 cup mild wine vinegar
1/2 teaspoon chili powder
Salt and pepper to taste

Place garbanzos, green onion, chiles, and pimientos in bowl. Mix other ingredients, then pour over bean mixture, tossing to coat. Chill 2 or 3 hours to allow flavors to mix. Serves 4.

Ensalada de Jícama y Naranja – **Jícama** and Orange Salad

Jícama is a root vegetable that looks like a brown, bumpy turnip. It has a mildly sweet, crunchy taste somewhat like a water chestnut. It is a favorite street food in Mexico, cut into thin strips, sprinkled with lime juice and chili powder, and served in paper cups. Jícama goes especially well with oranges. Here is a simple salad that is sure to please. When purchasing jícama, buy a smaller size for a sweeter taste. Avoid jícamas with soft spots or bruising on the outside.

1/2 head iceberg lettuce, thinly shredded
1 medium *jícama*, peeled, cut into thin rounds

3 large oranges, peeled, sliced into rounds
1 purple onion, cut into rings

(continued)

For the dressing, mix the following:

1/2 cup virgin olive oil
2 tablespoons lime or lemon juice
3 tablespoons wine vinegar

2 teaspoons chili powder
1 teaspoon salt

Arrange shredded lettuce on large plate. Place oranges and *jícama* slices in alternating rounds on lettuce. Place onion rings on top. Drizzle dressing over all. Serves 4 to 5.

Ixtapa-Zihuatanejo, Guerrero – Liberation of the Turtles

Hotels in the area particpate in collecting and protecting turtle eggs until they hatch and are ready to release. The releasing event gives hope for the survival of these endangered creatures.

Ensalada de Noche Buena – Christmas Eve Salad

This is one of the most famous salads in Mexico, traditionally served at the family dinner following midnight mass on Christmas Eve. Beets are a major ingredient in this salad along with colorful fruits, topped with pomegranate seeds. This spectacular salad will add a colorful touch to any buffet. It can be made ahead, adding the dressing just before serving.

1 can sliced beets
3 tablespoons sugar
2 bananas
1 red apple
1/4 pound *jícama* or added red apple

1 large orange
6 romaine lettuce leaves
4 tablespoons roasted peanuts,
    chopped
1/4 cup pomegranate seeds

(continued)

Dressing:

2 tablespoons sugar	3 tablespoons cider vinegar
1/4 teaspoon salt	

Place beets and beet liquid in pan with 3 tablespoons of sugar. Bring to a boil, lower heat, and simmer 5 minutes. Let beets cool in liquid, then pour off liquid and drain well. Put beets in refrigerator to chill.

Peel *jícama* and cut into thin slices. Leave apple peel on, but core apple and cut into thin slices. If salad is not going to be served right away, dip apple slices in lemon or lime juice mixed with an equal amount of water to prevent discoloration. Peel orange and cut into thin slices. Cut each slice in half. Peel bananas and cut into thin slices. Dip slices in lemon water to prevent discoloration. Shred the lettuce.

Line a large platter with the shredded lettuce. Arrange the *jícama*, orange, beet, apple, and banana slices in alternating circles or other patterns on the lettuce. Sprinkle with the peanuts. Top with the pomegranate seeds. In a small bowl, whisk 2 tablespoons sugar, salt, and vinegar until the sugar is dissolved. Drizzle over the salad just before serving. Makes 6 servings.

Older Mexican cookbooks call for cutting *jícama*, apple, oranges, bananas, and beets into chunks and combining with the nuts and pomegranate seeds. Enough liquid from the beets was added to the dressing to color the dressing a bright pink. Salad was tossed with dressing and arranged on lettuce leaves.

Note: The Spanish brought orange trees to Mexico in Colonial times. The climate and soil were ideally suited for growing oranges, which were quickly incorporated into Mexican cooking.

Ensalada de Rábanos – Radish Salad

Radishes were introduced to Mexico by the Spanish and quickly became a favorite vegetable used to garnish soups and main dishes. Radishes are often cut into rosettes with a few of the leaves still attached. Here is a tasty radish salad taken from an old Mexican cookbook.

6 bunches of red radishes, sliced
    or chopped
1 large tomato, chopped fine
1/4 cup onion, minced

1 teaspoon mint leaves, chopped
1/2 teaspoon salt
1/4 cup lime juice
2 tablespoons olive oil

Place radishes, tomato, and onion in a bowl. In another bowl, mix the mint leaves, salt, lime juice, and oil, stirring well. Pour over radishes and toss to mix. Spoon onto lettuce leaves. Serves 6.

Ensalada de Lechuga y Rábanos – Lettuce and Radish Salad

This salad goes well with all Mexican dishes and is a great garnish for tacos and tostadas.

4 cups packed shredded romaine lettuce
4 cups packed shredded iceberg lettuce
6 large radishes, grated
1/4 cup chopped cilantro

2 tablespoons fresh lime juice
1/4 cup olive oil
1/2 teaspoon salt

Place lettuces, radishes, and cilantro in large salad bowl. In a small bowl, combine lime juice, olive oil, and salt, mixing well. Pour dressing over the lettuces and toss lightly to mix. Makes 6 servings.

Ensalada Mexicana de Papa – Mexican Potato Salad

Here's a south-of-the-border recipe for potato salad. Try it for your next cookout.

2 pounds red potatoes
1 cup sliced carrots
1 small onion, chopped
1/4 cup chopped green onion
3 stalks celery, chopped
2 tablespoons chopped pickled
    jalapeño pepper

1 cup chicken stock
2 tablespoons white vinegar
2 tablespoons pickled jalapeño
    juice
3 tablespoons olive oil
1/2 teaspoon black pepper
1/2 teaspoon salt

Place potatoes in a saucepan and cover with water. Bring to a boil and cook until almost tender, about 15 minutes. Add carrots and cook until potatoes and carrots are tender. Drain and allow to cool. Peel and cube potatoes. Place potatoes, carrots, onion, celery, green onion, and pickled jalapeños into a large bowl. Combine the remaining ingredients, mixing well. Pour over potatoes and toss to mix. Serve at room temperature or slightly chilled. Serves 6.

Mexico City

Site of the once great Aztec civilization, Mexico City features 3,000 years of cultural life. It is one of the world's oldest cities with a metro-population of about 23 million. The city has five Aztec temples, the largest Catholic cathedral on the continent, and eleven ecological parks. Of note, is the Museum of Anthropology featuring the indigenous people of Mexico.

Salpicón – Shredded Meat Salad

This cold meat salad was introduced to Mexico by Spanish colonials. The Mexicans adapted the recipe adding local ingredients, such as chipotle in adobo sauce. This dish can be served as a salad course or makes a great buffet dish.

Meat:

3-1/2 to 4 pounds chuck, flank or
    brisket beef
1 large onion, quartered
3 cloves garlic, minced
1 teaspoon thyme

2 stalks celery
2 bay leaves
Salt and pepper to taste
2 quarts water

Place meat in heavy saucepan and cover with 2 quarts water. Add onion, garlic, thyme, celery stalks, bay leaves, and salt and pepper to taste. Bring to boil, cover and reduce heat. Simmer on low until meat is fork tender; 2-1/2 to 3 hours, adding water as needed. When cooked, let meat cool in liquid.

Salad:

Shredded meat

2 potatoes, cooked and cut into small cubes

1 cup diced Monterey Jack cheese

1 medium onion, thinly sliced

Mix the following to make the dressing:

1/2 cup olive oil

1/3 cup red wine vinegar

1 *chipotle*, finely chopped (from canned *chipotles* in *adobo* sauce)

2 teaspoons *adobo* sauce

1/2 teaspoon dry mustard

Salt and pepper to taste

Garnish:

6 to 8 radishes, sliced

Large lettuce leaves

3 avocados, cut in long slices

Ripe tomatoes, cut in thin wedges

(continued)

When meat is cool enough to handle, remove from liquid and place in glass bowl. Take two forks and working the forks against each other, pull the meat apart until it is in fine shreds. Add the cubed potatoes, cheese, and chopped onion, mixing well. Mix dressing ingredients together and pour over meat mixture. Toss lightly. Correct seasoning by adding more salt and pepper if needed. Cover and let stand in refrigerator for 3 or 4 hours or overnight.

To serve, arrange lettuce leaves on platter and heap meat salad in center. Garnish with avocado, radish, and tomato slices. Serve with warm tortillas or *bolillos* (Mexican crusty rolls) or sliced French bread. Makes 10 to 12 servings.

Ensalada de Nopalitos – Cactus Salad

Nopalitos *are the young shoots of the prickly pear cactus. The cactus paddles and cactus fruit have been popular foods in Mexico since prehistoric times. You can buy fresh cactus already prepared in the produce section of Latin-American markets. The whole leaves are also sold. These must be handled with tongs to protect your hands from the needles, and the needles must be removed before use. This recipe calls for the already-prepared cactus leaves. If you cannot find them, you can use canned cactus leaves, available in the Mexican food section.*

1 pound prepared *nopalitos*	1/4 cup olive oil
2 ripe tomatoes, chopped	2 tablespoons wine vinegar
1 small onion, chopped	Salt and pepper to taste
1/4 teaspoon oregano	1 tablespoon chopped cilantro

(continued)

Pickled jalapeño slices, for garnish

Rinse and drain the cactus. In bowl, combine *nopalitos*, tomato, onion, and oregano. Whisk oil, vinegar, salt and pepper together. Pour mixture over *nopalitos*, toss lightly to mix. Serve on individual plates on lettuce leaf. Sprinkle with cilantro and garnish with pickled jalapeño slices.

Mexico's Christmas Gift to the World

Old Spain provided many Christmas customs such as piñatas *and* posadas *but Mexico can claim the poinsettia as its own. The Aztecs called it* cuetlaxochitl, *the flower of purity. In 1825 the first U.S. Ambassador to Mexico, Dr. Joel Robert Poinsett, an amateur botanist, sent cuttings to his greenhouses in South Carolina. The plant bears his name.*

Verduras – Vegetables

Many of the common vegetables we eat today came from Mexico and Latin America: tomatoes, beans, squash, corn, potatoes, and avocados to name a few. When Mexicans eat vegetables, they like them well flavored with herbs, cheeses, and chiles.

La Noche de los Rábanos – The Night of the Radishes
In Oaxaca City, since 1895, as part of Christmas festivities, huge radishes are carved into fantastic shapes including nativity scenes, men riding horses, elephants, giraffes, bullfighters, devils, astronauts and more. No one eats these bitter tasting radishes. Figures are judged and prizes awarded, and winners are sold to the highest bidders.

Papas a la Mexicana – Mexican-Style Fried Potatoes

In the produce section of the Mexican markets, "White Rose" potatoes are sold. These are large potatoes with a very thin skin that can be rubbed off. This filling is commonly used in tacos and for breakfast burritos. Great with grilled beefsteak.

5 raw potatoes, sliced
3 tablespoons oil
1 onion, chopped
2 cloves garlic, minced

2 plum tomatoes, chopped
2 jalapeños, sliced
Salt and pepper to taste
1/2 cup grated Cheddar cheese

Sauté potatoes in oil. Add onion and garlic and cook 2 minutes. Add tomatoes and chiles. Let mixture fry well; add salt and pepper to taste. Cover and cook on low for 15 minutes. Remove cover, add cheese, and mix well. Serves 5.

Espinaca con Jalapeño – Jalapeño Spinach

This side dish goes well with grilled meats and fish and is easy to prepare.

2 bunches fresh spinach
1/2 cup water
1 teaspoon salt
2 (3-ounce) packages cream cheese

3 tablespoons finely chopped
    pickled jalapeño
2 to 3 tablespoons jalapeño
    liquid or white wine vinegar

Wash, stem, and roughly chop spinach. Place water and salt in skillet and bring to a boil. Add spinach, reduce heat to medium and cook for 4 to 5 minutes until spinach is tender. Add cream cheese, jalapeños, and jalapeño liquid. Reduce heat to simmer and cook until cheese is melted and coats spinach. Makes 6 servings.

Calabazas Rellenas – Stuffed Squash

Calabazas *are green striped squash grown in Mexico and available in Latin American markets in the United States. Zucchini can be substituted.*

6 to 9 squash
3 tablespoons butter
1 small onion, chopped fine
1 hard-boiled egg, chopped
1/2 cup cheese grated (Cheddar or
   Monterey Jack)

1 egg, beaten
Salt and pepper to taste
1/2 cup bread crumbs
1/2 cup cream

Select young, even-sized squash. Scoop out centers, leaving a thin wall. Mince the squash pulp. Melt butter in pan; add onion and cook until limp. Add squash pulp, hard-boiled egg, and cheese. Stir in beaten egg, and season with salt and pepper. Place filling in the squash shells and sprinkle with bread crumbs. Place in greased baking dish, dot with a little butter, and bake in 375° oven until tender, about 30 minutes. Baste the squash with cream. Serves 6.

Santuarios de la Mariposa Monarca
Monarch Butterfly Sanctuaries

In their annual migration, millions of butterflies from Canada and the United States land in several areas of the Oyamel forests near Angangueo, Michoacan. They hibernate in the winter and mate in the spring. Two sanctuaries are open for public viewing.

Calabaza con Elote – Squash with Corn

Zucchini can be substituted for the green-striped Mexican squash in this recipe.

1 small onion, chopped
2 tablespoons oil
2 cloves garlic
2 or 3 small green summer squash
2 large tomatoes, skinned and chopped

2 cups corn, cut off the cob, or 1 (1-pound) package frozen corn
1 (4-ounce) can chopped green chiles
Salt and pepper to taste
1/2 cup water

Heat oil in heavy saucepan, add onions, and cook until soft. Add garlic and cook a few more minutes. Add other ingredients and simmer until squash is soft.

Chiles en Nogada – Chiles in Walnut Sauce

Chiles en Nogada is Mexico's national dish. It was created by the people of Puebla, who served it to the victorious Mexican General Ignacio Zaragoza and his officers, following their defeat of French soldiers on May 5, 1862, at the Battle of Puebla. The dish is made of green chiles, stuffed with savory meat filling, covered in a white sauce and garnished with red pomegranate seeds and comprises the three colors of the Mexican flag. It is served for special occasions and was featured at the wedding banquet in the book "Like Water for Chocolate," *a 1989 novel by Laura Esquivel. The book is a bestseller in many languages.*

8 fresh *poblano* chiles
Roast the chiles directly over a gas flame or under the broiler until they are

(continued)

browned and blistered. Place in paper bag or wrap in a tea towel to sweat for about 20 minutes. The heat will cause the skin to loosen during this process. Peel off the skin. Make a slit in the side of each chile and remove the seeds and membranes, being careful to leave top part and stem. Rinse and pat dry.

Picadillo – **Meat Filling:**

2 tablespoons oil
1 onion, chopped
2 garlic cloves, minced
1 pound lean ground beef
1 teaspoon cinnamon
1 teaspoon cumin
1/4 cup raisins
2 tablespoons chopped green olives
2 tablespoons chopped candied fruit (citron or pineapple)
1/4 cup chopped pecans or pine nuts
Salt and pepper to taste

Brown the onion and garlic in oil, cooking until limp, add other ingredients.

Cook until meat is cooked through and starts to brown. Set aside to cool, then stuff chiles with this mixture. If slit will not close, use a toothpick.

Frying Batter:

6 eggs, separated   Oil for frying
1/2 cup flour

In large bowl, beat egg whites until stiff peaks form. In another bowl, beat egg yolks until creamy. Fold egg yolks into egg whites, mixing well. Fold in about 2 tablespoons of the flour. Heat oil with about 1/4-inch depth in a skillet. Dust chiles with a little of the flour. Carefully pick up stuffed chile, dip in egg mixture, and place chile in hot oil. Tilt pan to coat chiles as much as possible to avoid handling. When golden brown, carefully turn over and cook on other side. Remove and drain on paper towels. Keep warm in 150° oven until all are done.

(continued)

Walnut Cream Sauce:

1 cup milk	1 to 2 tablespoons sugar
1/2 cup *queso fresco* or cream cheese	Seeds of 1 pomegranate
1/2 cup chopped walnuts	Chopped cilantro, for garnish

Heat the milk and cheese on very low heat to prevent burning. When cheese is melted, add the sugar and walnuts, remove from heat and allow to cool to room temperature. To serve, place a stuffed chile on each plate and cover with the walnut sauce (the *Nogada*). Sprinkle with pomegranate seeds. Garnish plate with chopped cilantro. Makes 8 servings.

Note: So celebrated is this dish, it appears in competitions including those at the Chile in Walnut Sauce Festival in Puebla.

Frijoles Básicos – Basic Beans

Beans are a major food in the Mexican diet and are usually served with every meal. The light brown speckled pinto beans are most commonly used. The traditional Mexican way of preparing them is to cook them in a clay pot over a slow fire. You can get the same effect by placing the beans in a slow cooker.

1 pound dry pinto beans	Water to cover beans
2 or 3 cloves garlic	1 tablespoon bacon drippings
1 onion, sliced	Salt to taste

Rinse beans briefly in hot water. Place in heavy pot or slow cooker, adding all ingredients except salt. For stove top method, bring beans to boil, lower heat and cover. Simmer on low until beans are soft (2 to 3 hours). In slow cooker, use high setting, cooking for 5 to 6 hours. Add salt to taste and cook 15 minutes more.

Frijoles Refritos – Refried Beans

Here is the bean dish most commonly associated with Mexico. Refried beans are served as an appetizer, with breakfast eggs, on sandwiches (tortas), *and with the main meal.*

2 cups cooked pinto beans
3 tablespoons oil

1/2 cup bean liquid or water
1/2 cup grated Cheddar or
Monterey Jack cheese

Heat oil in heavy skillet. Add beans and stir and mash as they cook. Add liquid to beans as needed. Continue mashing beans until a smooth paste is formed. Cook on low until liquid is absorbed. Sprinkle cheese on top when serving. Serves 6.

Frijoles Charros – Cowboy Beans

1 pound dried pinto beans
6 bacon strips, chopped
2 onions, chopped
4 garlic cloves, minced
4 fresh jalapeños, stemmed and chopped
4 tomatoes, chopped

1/2 cup chopped thinly sliced ham
4 green onions, chopped
1/2 cup chopped cilantro leaves
1/2 chicken boullion cube
Salt to taste

Rinse beans in a colander under hot water 2 or 3 minutes. Place beans in large saucepan and add water to cover. Add bacon, onion, garlic, jalapeños, tomatoes, and ham. Bring to boil, cover and reduce heat. Simmer on low heat until beans are almost done (about 1-1/2 hours). Add green onions and chopped cilantro. Add boullion cube and salt to taste. Simmer another 30 minutes. Serve beans in bowl with broth.

Tamales de Elote – Green Corn Tamales

These tamales are best when made with freshly picked corn. If leaves are stiff and hard to fold, place in microwave about 30 seconds to soften.

6 large ears fresh sweet corn
1-1/2 teaspoons salt
1 (4-ounce) can chopped green chiles

1 cup grated Cheddar cheese
1/2 cup butter, melted
1/2 cup *masa* or corn meal

Cut kernels off corn; reserve leaves. Place half of corn in food processor; process until smooth. In a large bowl, mix processed corn with remaining corn, then add other ingredients and stir until well mixed.

Wash leaves well and place about 2 tablespoons of corn mixture in the center of each leaf. Fold edges of leaf over mixture and place tamal, folded edges down, in steamer. Once all tamales are stacked in steamer, steam for about 40 minutes until corn mixture is done. Makes 8 servings.

Sopas Secas – Dry Soups

Mexico has a category of soups called *Sopas Secas* or dry soups. These are rice and pasta dishes which were introduced to Mexico by Spanish and Chinese immigrants. No one knows why these dishes are called dry soups, but it may be due to the early native languages which did not have a single word for eating, but many words describing the state of food you were eating, such as eating soft food, eating crisp food, eating sour food. These dishes were new and served like soup, but without liquid, hence dry soup. When *sopa seca* is served at the *comida*, the main meal of the day, it is served as the second course, following soup. More recently, the dry soup is being added to the main course.

Sopa de Fideo – Vermicelli Soup

8 ounces vermicelli
3 or 4 tablespoons bacon drippings
1/2 medium onion, chopped
1 clove garlic, finely minced
2 medium tomatoes, chopped

1 chicken boullion cube
Salt and pepper to taste
2 cups water
2 cups water
Parmesan cheese, optional

Cook the vermicelli in the bacon drippings until lightly browned, stirring to prevent burning. Add remaining ingredients and simmer until liquid is absorbed, about 25 minutes. You can sprinkle a little fresh-grated parmesan cheese on top before serving. Makes 4 to 6 servings.

Rice Cooking Tips

Mexican rice should be dry when served with each grain of rice standing by itself. Here is a quick summary on how to soak and wash rice, plus tips for making perfect Mexican rice:

Use the correct type of rice: You need long grain white rice that is not "converted" or precooked in any way. Do not use pearl rice, this rice has too much starch.

Soak and rinse the rice: Put the raw rice in a bowl of hot water and soak for about 15 minutes. Then drain in a sieve and rinse with cold water until the water runs clear. Let drain for 10 minutes before frying.

Do not stir: Once you have put the liquid in the rice, bring it to a boil,

 (continued)

then turn it low to simmer; do not stir. Let the liquid cook away, then fluff the rice with a fork.

Soak up extra liquid: Here is another trick from one of Diana Kennedy's books. If all the liquid is not absorbed and you don't want to overcook the rice, lay a terry cloth towel over the top of the hot rice (after it is removed from the burner). Pull the towel tight so it does not rest on the rice. The towel will absorb the excess moisture from the rice.

Fry the rice: Put the drained raw rice in a hot skillet with oil and fry until golden brown. The frying will impart a nutty taste to the rice.

Mexican Saying

La cobija de los pobres—El Sol.   The blanket of the poor—The Sun.

Arroz a la Mexicana – Mexican Rice

This recipe is for the classic dish served in Mexican restaurants and is also called Spanish Rice.

2 cups long grain rice
1/4 cup oil
1 medium onion, diced
3 cloves garlic, finely minced
3 ripe tomatoes, peeled and chopped

1 fresh jalapeño pepper, chopped
1 chicken boullion cube
3 cups water
Salt to taste

Presoak and wash rice as described in rice cooking tips on page 87. Heat oil in heavy skillet, add the drained rice, and fry about 5 minutes. Add onions and continue frying until rice is golden, about 2 more minutes. Add garlic and cook

(continued)

one minute more. Add other ingredients and stir to mix. Bring to boil, then reduce heat to low simmer. Cover and let cook for about 15 minutes. Turn off heat and let rice stand covered until all the liquid is absorbed. Before serving, fluff with a fork. Makes 6 to 8 servings.

Arroz Blanco – White Rice

Make rice as for Mexican rice, omitting the tomatoes and jalapeño peppers. Replace tomatoes with 1/2 cup frozen peas and 1/2 cup finely chopped carrots for color.

Arroz Verde – Green Rice

2 cups long grain rice	1/2 cup water
5 ounces fresh spinach	1/4 cup oil

1/3 cup fresh parsley	3 cups water or chicken broth
1/3 cup chopped cilantro	Salt to taste
1 small onion, chopped	2 or 3 *poblano* chiles, roasted
2 cloves garlic, finely minced	peeled and cut into strips

Soak rice and rinse as described in rice cooking tips on page 88. Rinse spinach and place in saucepan with no water added. Cover and cook for five minutes. Place cooked spinach in blender or food processor with parsley, cilantro, onion, garlic, and 1/2 cup water. Purée until smooth, then set aside. Heat oil in heavy skillet and add rice, frying until light and golden brown. Add the spinach purée to rice; cook for 2 minutes. Add the water or chicken broth and salt to taste. Let the rice boil, lower heat, cover, cook for 20 minutes. Allow rice to stand until liquid is absorbed. Garnish with *poblano* strips when serving. Serves 6 to 8.

Sopas y Caldos – Soups and Stews

Mexicans love their soup and serve it as the first course of the *comida*, their main meal served in the middle of the day. Many of the soups served in Mexico have their roots in Spanish cuisine, such as garlic soup and vegetable stews, but many are of Mexican origin like *pozole* and tortilla soup. Just as other Mexican foods are often served with fresh food garnishes, soup is usually accompanied by chopped avocados, sliced radishes, limes, and cheese to add to the soup just before eating.

Crema de Elote – Cream of Corn Soup

1 tomato, chopped
1 onion, chopped
4 tablespoons butter
1 (10-ounce) bag frozen corn kernels
1 (4-ounce) can chopped green chiles

4 cups milk
1 chicken bouillon cube
Pinch baking soda
1 small can evaporated milk
1 cup white Cheddar cheese
Salt and pepper to taste

Place tomato and onion in blender or food processor and blend until smooth. Melt butter in large saucepan, add corn and sauté until cooked. Add tomato mixture and green chiles, mixing well. Add milk, bouillon cube, and baking soda, and bring to boil, stirring to dissolve the bouillon cube. Simmer on low for 15 minutes. Add the evaporated milk and cheese, and simmer for 3 minutes more. Add salt and pepper to taste.

Sopa de Tortilla – Tortilla Soup

Tortilla soup is Mexico's most famous soup and is a standard menu item in most Mexican restaurants in the United States. It is easy to make and so satisfying. You can add as many garnishes as you like, just a as long as you include crisp tortilla strips and chopped avocado.

3 tablespoons oil
1 onion, finely chopped
2 cloves garlic, finely minced
6 cups chicken stock
1 (16-ounce) can puréed tomatoes

1 cup cooked chicken, chopped
  (optional)
2 tablespoons finely chopped
  pickled jalapeño pepper
Salt and pepper to taste

In heavy pan heat oil to medium high, add chopped onions and cook until soft and clear. Add garlic and cook for another minute. Add chicken stock, tomatoes, chopped chicken, and jalapeños. Season the soup with salt and pepper. Bring to a boil, then reduce heat and simmer on low for about 30 minutes.

Serve in bowls with the following garnishes:

Corn tortillas cut in thin strips and fried crisp	Grated Monterey Jack cheese
Chopped avocado	Fresh lime slices

Mexican Saying
Aunque la mona se vista de seda, mona se queda.
Even though the monkey dresses in silk, she is still a monkey.

Sopa de Albóndigas – Meatball Soup

This is another classic Mexican soup, almost a meal in a bowl.

Broth:

2 tablespoons oil	3 carrots, sliced thin
1 onion, diced	2 or 3 stalks celery, sliced thin
2 cloves garlic, diced	1/2 teaspoon dried oregano
1 (16-ounce) can diced tomatoes	1 teaspoon ground cumin
2 or 3 jalapeños, sliced thin	2 quarts water

In large soup pot, brown onion and garlic in oil until limp. Add other ingredients and bring to a boil, reduce to simmer and cook while preparing meatballs.

Meatballs

2 pounds lean ground beef
3 eggs
1 cup uncooked long grain rice
1/4 onion, finely chopped

1/2 teaspoon ground cumin
    powder
1 tablespoon chopped fresh mint
    or 1 teaspoon dried mint
1/4 cup chopped cilantro

Except for cilantro, mix ingredients well and form into small meatballs about the size of walnuts. Drop meatballs into simmering broth, cover, and cook for about 30 minutes. Turn off heat and allow to stand 5 minutes, then stir in cilantro. Serve in soup bowls with cheese and chopped avocado for garnish along with warm tortillas.

Sopa de Flor de Calabaza – Squash Blossom Soup

Squash blossoms are a favorite ingredient in Mexican cooking. If you have ever grown squash in your garden, you know that you will have an abundance of these blossoms. This recipe makes a beautiful pale, golden soup. If you do not have any squash blossoms, use yellow crookneck squash.

3 tablespoons butter
1 onion, chopped
1 quart squash blossoms

2 tablespoons flour
4 cups milk or cream
Salt and pepper to taste

Gather squash blossoms:
Each morning gather the male flowers from the plants. Male flowers do not have a tiny fruit behind the flower.

Rinse and shake off water, then store in plastic bag in refrigerator until you have one quart.

Soup:
Heat butter in skillet, add onion and squash blossoms. Sauté until onions and flowers are limp. Place in blender or food processor and blend along with the flour and milk. Return to heat and cook until thickened, stirring to prevent scorching. Add salt and pepper to taste. Serve with croutons for garnish. Makes 4 servings.

Fiesta de la Virgen de Guadalupe – **Day of the Virgin of Guadalupe**
Millions come to the Mexico City Basilica on December 12, to pay homage to the nation's patron saint. This is the most important religious holiday in all of Mexico.

Sopa de Limón – Lime Soup

This tart and refreshing soup, from the Yucatán, is perfect for a summer day. Serve with plenty of fresh lime slices.

2 whole chicken breasts
2 quarts water
2 or 3 chicken boullion cubes
Juice from 3 fresh limes
2 tomatoes, peeled and chopped
1 sprig *epazote*

3 or 4 sprigs cilantro
1 *guerro* or red dried chile
2 *habanero* chiles
Juice from 1 lemon
6 corn tortillas, cut into strips
    and fried

Cook the chicken breasts in water with boullion cubes, lime juice, tomatoes, sprigs of cilantro, *epazote,* and the *guerro* or red dried chile. When chicken is cooked, remove from heat and let cool. Shred the meat and return to broth, bring to a boil and simmer on low heat for 10 more minutes. Add salt to taste. Make a *habanero* sauce by roasting the *habanero* chiles, then chopping fine, adding lemon juice. Serve the soup with fried tortilla strips, *habanero* sauce, and fresh lime slices.

Editor's note: Epazote *is a herb native to southern Mexico, Central America, and South America. It is similar to the licorice taste of anise, fennel, or tarragon, but stronger. Arturo Medina writes,* "Epazote *can be added to any of the bean recipes."*

Pozole – Pork and Hominy Soup

This hardy soup comes from the state of Jalisco and is served at parties and Independence Day dinners on September 15. With all the fresh vegetable garnishes, it is like eating soup and salad in one bowl, and it is a delicious combination.

1 pound boneless pork, cut
  into 1-inch pieces
4 cups water
4 *ancho* chiles, stemmed
  and seeded
2 cloves garlic
1 teaspoon Mexican oregano

2 tablespoons vegetable oil
1 large onion, diced
2 cups yellow hominy,
  drained well
3 cups pork or chicken stock
  as needed
Salt and pepper to taste

Garnishes
Sliced radishes, shredded lettuce or cabbage, diced onion, fried corn tortilla strips, diced avocado, and lime slices.

Sprinkle pork with salt and pepper and put into pan with water. Bring to boil, and simmer uncovered until barely tender, about 30 minutes. Remove from heat and let the pork cool. Drain meat and reserve liquid. Set aside, covering with damp towel. Place the *ancho* chiles in the reserved cooking liquid and let soak for twenty minutes. Transfer liquid and chiles to a blender or food processor. Add garlic and oregano. Purée until smooth and set aside.

In a heavy saucepan over medium heat, warm oil. Add onion and sauté until golden, about 10 minutes. Add chile purée, hominy, and pork or chicken stock, adding more stock for a more soupy consistency. Stir in pork. Bring to boil, then lower heat to medium low and simmer uncovered until pork is fork tender, about 30 minutes. Adjust seasonings. Serve in shallow bowl and pass garnishes. Makes 4 to 6 servings.

Sopa de Lechuga – Lettuce Soup

A recipe for this soup was found in a 1962 cookbook from Villa Montaña, a small hotel in the colonial city of Morelia, which opened for business in 1953 and is still in operation today. Villa Montaña is known as one of the most romantic hotels in Mexico and is a favorite honeymoon destination for newly-weds from Mexico City. Every room is uniquely decorated. The lettuce soup continues to be a popular menu item. Here is a simple version of this tasty soup.

4 cups romaine lettuce, chopped
1 cup water
1 tablespoon butter
1 tablespoon onion, chopped
2-1/2 cups chicken stock

1/2 cup cream or evaporated milk
1/4 teaspoon nutmeg
Salt and pepper to taste
Croutons for garnish

Cook lettuce with 1 cup water until lettuce is tender. Place cooked lettuce with water in food processor or blender, and process, leaving a little leaf texture. Brown the onion in butter. To a large soup pan, add lettuce, onion, and stock. Bring to a boil, then lower to a slow simmer. Stir in cream, nutmeg, salt and pepper. Simmer on low for 10 to 15 minutes. Serve with croutons. Makes 6 servings.

Mexican Riddle

En lo alto vive,	It lives way up,
en lo alto mora.	way up it dwells.
En lo alto teje	Up there it weaves
la tejedora.	a weaver's spell.
La Araña	The Spider

Sopa de Ajo – Garlic Soup

This soup was introduced by Spanish settlers, and is now a favorite in Mexico.

2 tablespoons olive oil	3/4 cup dry bread crumbs
30 peeled garlic cloves (about 3 bulbs)	6 cups chicken stock
1/4 cup water	2 eggs

Heat oil in a large heavy pan. Add garlic and sauté, stirring constantly until golden brown, about 8 minutes. Remove garlic and reserve the oil.

Place garlic in blender with the water, purée and set aside. Brown the bread crumbs in the reserved oil. Add the chicken stock and garlic purée, and simmer for 15 minutes. In a small bowl, beat the eggs. Bring the soup to a rolling boil and pour the eggs in a stream into the soup, stirring constantly. Lower heat and simmer for 5 minutes more. Let stand a few minutes. Serves 6.

Pollo y Pavo – Poultry

The turkey is native to Mexico and was domesticated by the Mexican natives long before Cortez arrived in their land. Spanish colonials introduced chickens to Mexico and soon they became an important food source for the native population.   ·

Arturo Medina adds: *Semi-domesticated turkeys called* guajolotes *in Mexico have darker meat and taste gamier than domestic turkeys.* Guajolote *in* mole *sauce* is a very traditional dish served at wedding banquets.*

*See page 117

Pavo Relleno – Stuffed Turkey

Cortez took the turkey to Spain where it quickly became a favorite food of the wealthy classes. Within a few years, turkeys were being sold in markets all over Europe. The name "turkey" comes from England, where Turkish merchants first sold turkeys. The English called the bird "turkey chicken," which was later shortened to turkey. This recipe is prepared for fiestas and special events.

1 (10 to 12-pound) turkey
1/2 pound dried apples
1/2 cup chopped prunes
1 cup raisins
1 tablespoon oil

1/2 pound chorizo sausage
1 small onion, chopped
1/4 cup pine nuts
1 clove garlic, finely minced
1/4 cup chopped parsley

1/4 cup finely chopped ham	1 teaspoon oregano
1/2 teaspoon thyme	Salt
1 cup sherry	Garlic powder

Rub inside of turkey with salt and set aside. Soak apples, prunes, and raisins in water for 15 minutes; drain. Heat oil in skillet. Add ham and crumbled sausage, browning well. Add fruits, pine nuts, onion, garlic, parsley, oregano, and thyme. Cook slowly for about 15 minutes. Add sherry and simmer until liquid has evaporated. Allow mixture to cool. Stuff the turkey with the filling. Place turkey in greased roasting pan. Rub outside of turkey with salt and garlic powder. Roast in 350° oven, allowing 30 minutes per pound. Remove from oven and allow to stand for 15 minutes before slicing. Serves 12 to 15.

Pollo en Salsa Verde – Chicken in Green Sauce

Salsa Verde* *has a base made of* tomatillos, *a small green fruit popular in Mexican cooking. The tartness of the* tomatillos *goes well with the mild taste of chicken.*

8 boneless chicken breast halves
2 cups green sauce or 2 (4-ounce) cans
    prepared *salsa verde**
1 cup sour cream

1 cup grated Monterey Jack
    cheese
1/4 cup sliced pickled jalapeño
    peppers

Place chicken breasts in shallow baking dish. Pour green sauce over chicken, dot sour cream on top. Sprinkle the cheese over top and then scatter pickled jalapeño slices on top. Bake in 350° oven for 25 to 30 minutes, until sauce is bubbling and chicken is cooked. Makes 6 servings.   *See page 44

Pollo en Comino – Cumin Chicken

This is a classic dish from Guanajuato. Serve with an orange and jícama *salad.*

1 fryer chicken, cut into
   serving pieces
Juice of 2 oranges
Juice of 2 lemons
1/3 cup tequila

1 teaspoon cinnamon
1/4 teaspoon cloves
1 teaspoon cumin seeds,
   lightly toasted
3 tablespoons olive oil
1 teaspoon salt

For 8 serving pieces of chicken, you will need 2 thighs, 2 drumsticks, 2 breast halves, cut in half crosswise. Other pieces such as back, neck, and wings can be used for soup stock. Using a skewer or toothpick, punch holes in the skin all

(continued)

over the chicken pieces. In a small bowl, mix the orange juice, lemon juice, tequila, cinnamon, and cloves to make a marinade.

Place the chicken in a shallow dish and pour marinade over the chicken, turning pieces to coat. Sprinkle with toasted cumin seeds, cover and marinate in refrigerator, two to four hours, turning the chicken occasionally.

Remove chicken from marinade and pat dry. Heat oil to medium high and add chicken pieces. Season with salt and cook until brown on all sides, about 15 to 20 minutes. Pour in the marinade; reduce heat to simmer and cover, cooking another 30 minutes until the chicken is cooked through. The juices should be dark golden and coat the meat nicely.

Note: To toast the cumin, place seeds in a dry skillet heated to medium-high and stir constantly until lightly browned (about 2 minutes).

Pollo a la Naranja – Orange Chicken

The Spanish brought orange trees to Mexico in colonial times. The climate and soil were ideally suited for growing oranges, which were quickly incorporated into Mexican cooking. This is a classic Mexican dish.

4 chicken breasts, cut in half
1/2 cup flour
1 teaspoon salt
1/2 teaspoon pepper
4 tablespoons oil
1 small onion, chopped
2 or 3 garlic cloves, minced
1/2 cup slivered almonds

1 cup orange juice
1/4 cup raisins
1/2 cup crushed pineapple, drained
1/2 teaspoon cinnamon
1/8 teaspoon cloves
1 cup white wine
Orange slices, for garnish

(continued)

Coat chicken breasts in flour, salt and pepper mixture. Heat oil in heavy skillet and brown chicken breasts in oil. Place in baking dish. Sauté onion, garlic, and almonds in same oil. When onions are soft, add orange juice, raisins, pineapple, and spices and simmer a few minutes, then pour over chicken. Cover and bake in 325° oven for 35 to 40 minutes. Uncover chicken and turn. Add wine, basting well. Increase temperature and bake 15 minutes. Garnish chicken with orange slices when serving. Makes 4 servings.

A Mexican Riddle

Advinia, adivinanza,	Guess what it is,
que se pela por la panza?	that loses its skin?
La naranja.	The orange.

Arroz con Pollo – Chicken with Rice

There are many versions of this popular Latin American recipe. Here is an easy-to-make recipe that is sure to please.

Poach one chicken in water with bay leaf, onion, salt and pepper. Remove meat from bones and cut into bite-sized pieces. Reserve chicken poaching liquid.

1 cup uncooked long grain rice	1/2 teaspoon paprika
3 tablespoons oil	1/2 teaspoon pepper
1 onion, chopped	3 or 4 Roma tomatoes, chopped
3 cloves garlic, chopped and mashed	2 cups chicken stock
with one teaspoon salt	1/2 cup bell pepper slices

(continued)

Sauté rice in oil in a heavy skillet. Fry golden brown. Add the onion, garlic, and cook until onions are soft. Add tomatoes and chicken stock; season with paprika and pepper. Bring to a boil, then lower heat. Place the chicken pieces and bell pepper slices on the rice. Cover and cook on low until all moisture is absorbed (about 30 minutes). Serve with corn tortillas and guacamole.

The *Pocho* Dance, Tenosique, Tabasco

The dances begin at the church January 20, in the main park in Tenosique. These ceremonial dances of ancient origin are performed by masked dancers, who may be dressed as jaguars and tigers. The dances symbolize the dual battles of good and evil resulting in the purification of man. The dancers perform on Sundays before Ash Wednesday and carnival time. On the last day, they dance backwards from the main square to the church.

Mole Poblano – Chicken or Turkey *Mole*

This is one of the most famous of all Mexican recipes.

4 cups cooked turkey or chicken meat
1 (8-1/2-ounce) jar dark *mole*
1 tablespoon smooth peanut butter
1 tablespoon sugar
1 square dark unsweetened chocolate

4 cups chicken broth
1 cup tomato purée
1 teaspoon vinegar
Salt to taste
1/2 cup toasted almonds,
  for garnish

Remove *mole* sauce from jar and place in large saucepan. Warm the sauce over low heat, stirring constantly to keep from burning. Add broth to make a smooth paste and simmer for 15 minutes. Add tomato purée, peanut butter, sugar, chocolate, and vinegar. Add salt as needed. Cook and stir for 20 minutes.

(continued)

Add the chicken or turkey and simmer until meat is thoroughly heated, about 8 to 10 minutes. Place in serving dish, garnish with almonds. Serve over rice with warm tortillas.

Legend says that this dish originated in the state of Puebla in the Santa Clara Convent during the 17th century. The nuns were preparing a banquet for the visiting archbishop when the mole *sauce was developed. The legend has several versions: the nuns spilling spices and chocolate on the turkey, a native woman helping make the sauce, or a bare cupboard forcing the nuns to make do with ingredients on hand. Whatever its origin, making* mole *takes all day, toasting, grinding, and mixing ingredients. Luckily, you can buy prepared* mole *sauce.* Mole *paste will stay fresh in the freezer for several months. A* mole *fair and competition with thousands of entries is held annually near Mexico City.*

Pollo Yucatán – Yucatán Grilled Chicken

Cooks from the Yucatán like to use achiote *paste or powder made of seeds from the fruit of the* achiote *tree. The seeds produce a pigment called* annatto, *which is used to color food to a bright orange color. Early natives mixed the* achiote *with chocolate for a drink. The Spaniards were horrified to see their orange lips and tongues after tasting the liquid. Today, it is used for flavoring and natural food coloring. You can find the* achiote *paste or the Sason Seasoning™ (a mixture of* achiote *and seasonings) in the Mexican food section of your supermarket.*

2 (3-pound) fryers, cut in half

(continued)

Marinade

Mix the following:

Juice of 3 oranges

Juice of 1 lime

1 tablespoon oil

3 teaspoons *achiote* paste, or

    2 packs Sason Mix™

3 cloves garlic, mashed fine

Salt and pepper to taste

Place chicken halves in shallow dish and pour marinade over chicken. Marinate 4 to 5 hours. Drain meat, reserving marinade. Cook chicken on grill over hot coals until cooked through, brushing chicken with marinade while it is cooking. Serve with *Charro* (Cowboy) beans, salsa, and flour tortillas.

Budín Azteca – Aztec Pudding

2 whole chicken breasts (bone in)
1 small chopped onion
4 *poblano* or Anaheim green chiles,
    roasted, skinned with seeds and
    veins removed (divided use)
2 tablespoons oil

2 tomatoes chopped
1 cup sour cream
8 to 10 corn tortillas cut into
    quarters
1 cup grated Monterey Jack cheese
Chopped green onion, for garnish

Cover chicken breasts with water; season with salt and pepper. Simmer until cooked, about 25 minutes. Remove chicken, debone and shred, reserving broth.

Dice one of the green chiles. In a skillet, sauté the onion and chiles in the oil about five minutes. Add tomatoes and chicken, cook a few minutes, then remove from heat. *(continued)*

In a blender or food processor, purée the remaining 3 chiles with sour cream and 1/2 cup of the chicken broth to make a thin sauce. Oil or spray a 9 x 11-inch baking dish. Place a layer of half of the tortilla pieces in baking dish, followed by the chicken mixture, top with a layer of remaining half of the tortilla pieces. Pour the green chile sauce over dish. Top with grated cheese. Bake in 400° oven for 35 minutes. Serve garnished with chopped green onion.

A Proud History

Pre-Columbian Aztecs coming to the valley of Mexico saw a good omen: a large eagle with a snake in its talons, perched on a giant cactus. This is now the site of Mexico City. The eagle holding the snake is a national symbol which is centered in the flag.

Carne – Meat

When the Spanish came to Mexico, they brought cows, sheep, pigs, and goats to the natives. Prior to the Spanish invasion, native dishes used wild game and exotic forest animals for their meat protein. Pork and beef were quickly adapted to native recipes and new recipes were developed by inventive cooks.

Fusionamieto de los Toros – Running of the Bulls
San Miguel de Allende is host to this event in September on the weekend between Independence Day (September 16) and the festival for the city's patron saint, San Miguel el Arcángel (September 29). Over 200,000 particpants come to this annual event. A dozen or more specially raised bulls are set loose, barricaded in the townsquare, and joined by many people dressed in red bandanas and white shirts.

Fajitas – Grilled Skirt Steak

Some food historians say fajitas *originated in South Texas, but it is more likely that this dish originated on the cattle ranches in northern Mexico. The skirt steak is considered to be an inferior cut and was part of the meat scraps given to the* vaqueros *(cowboys) when cattle were butchered for the rancher's family. The* vaqueros *would build an open fire and grill the meat, serving it with flour tortillas.*

1 (3-pound) beef skirt steak
1 onion, sliced

1 bell pepper, sliced
1 tomato, sliced

Marinade:

Juice of 4 or 5 limes
3 or 4 garlic cloves, finely minced
4 tablespoons Worcestershire sauce

2 tablespoons salad oil
Salt and pepper to taste

Place beef skirt steak in shallow dish. Pour marinade over meat and refrigerate 3 or 4 hours. Place sliced onion, bell pepper, and tomato in marinade.

To cook meat, remove from marinade and place on grill over hot coals and cook as desired. Just before meat is finished cooking, place vegetables on grill and cook briefly. Cut meat into thin slices, being sure to cut across the grain. Serve with grilled vegetables, *pico de gallo*, and warm flour tortillas.

Albóndigas en Chipotle – Meat Balls in *Chipotle* Sauce

This recipe calls for a can of chipotles *in* adobo *sauce, found in the Mexican food section at the supermarket.* Chipotle *chiles impart a rich smoky flavor to this dish. Use these chiles sparingly, as they are hot!*

Meatballs:

1 pound lean ground beef
1 cup bread crumbs
1 egg
2 cloves garlic, finely minced

1 teaspoon pepper
1/2 teaspoon salt
1/2 small onion, grated
1 tablespoon Worcestershire
sauce

Mix all ingredients well and shape into small walnut-sized meatballs.

Bake at 375° in shallow pan, sprayed with non-stick cooking spray for 15 to 20 minutes. Turn once while baking so meatballs brown on all sides.

Chipotle Sauce:

2 tablespoons oil
1 clove garlic, finely minced
1 slice dry bread, crumbled
3 canned *chipotle* chiles

3 tablespoons *adobo* sauce from chiles
1 can tomato sauce
2 cups stock or water

Heat oil in skillet; sauté garlic a minute or so, then add bread crumbs, and fry until lightly toasted.

Purée *chipotle*, add *adobo* sauce, bread and garlic mixture, and tomato sauce. Pour puréed mixture into skillet or large saucepan. Add stock or water, and bring to full-simmer. Add meatballs and simmer on low about 20 to 25 minutes. Serves 4.

Chili con Carne a la Mexicana – Mexican Chili with Meat

Here is a Mexican version of that Texas favorite, Chili – Bowl of Red.

2 pounds stew meat, cut into small cubes	10 California dry chile pods
1/4 cup oil	4 cloves garlic
Salt to taste	3 cups water
2 cooked potatoes, cubed	1/2 teaspoon oregano

Fry the beef in cooking oil, salt to taste, add potatoes and cook a few minutes longer. Soak the chile pods in hot water for 10 minutes. Remove stems and seeds. Blend chiles with garlic and water. Strain mixture and pour into fried meat and potatoes. Let mixture come to a boil, then lower heat and simmer 25 to 30 minutes. Add oregano 5 minutes before serving. Serves 6 to 7.

Bistec a la Mexicana – Mexican-Style Sirloin Tips

3 teaspoons oil
1 pound of beef sirloin, cubed small
1 onion, chopped
2 cloves garlic, finely minced

2 tomatoes, chopped
2 to 3 fresh jalapeños, seeds and
     top removed, sliced crosswise
Salt and pepper to taste

In a heavy skillet, heat oil until very hot. Add meat and cook until brown. Add onion and garlic and cook until onion is transparent. Add tomatoes and jalapeños, sauté until cooked. Add a little water if needed. Add salt and pepper to taste. Serve immediately. Serves 4 to 5.

Carne Seca – Beef Jerky

This meat is the Mexican version of beef jerky. It is used by pounding the dried strips, then incorporating into recipes. The meat is used in tacos and in a classic Mexican dish, popular in northern Mexico, scrambled eggs with carne seca.

3 pounds lean beef
1/2 cup steak sauce

1/2 cup lemon juice
Salt and pepper

Slice meat into thin strips, with grain (lengthwise). Place in a shallow dish, cover with steak sauce and lemon juice. Marinate 4 to 6 hours or overnight. Remove meat and sprinkle with salt and pepper. Place on baking rack and bake in oven 9 to 12 hours at 140°. If you do not have a roasting pan with a rack, use oven rack and cover bottom of oven with aluminum foil.

Cinco de Mayo – Fifth of May

Cinco de Mayo *celebrates the Battle of Puebla, which occurred on May 5, 1862. A courageous group of Mexican soldiers, led by General Ignacio Zaragoza, defeated well-armed and trained French soldiers sent by Napoleon III to take control of Mexico. The battle showed the courage and determination of the Mexican people to be free of foreign rule.*

Cinco de Mayo *is more popular in the United States among Mexican immigrants than in Mexico. Towns along the U.S. and Mexican border celebrated the event, and this tradition soon spread to most large American cities with organized parades. Many Americans do not know that* Cinco de Mayo *is not Mexico's Independence Day, which is on September 16 and is a major holiday in Mexico.*

Tinga Poblana – Puebla Stew

Serve this easy-to-make authentic Mexican dish from the state of Puebla for a Cinco de Mayo *celebration. The recipe is a hardy pork dish which can be served on crisp tostados. It is a favorite street food in the market places.*

2 pounds lean pork meat
1 whole clove garlic
2 bay leaves
1/2 pound chorizo sausage
1 small onion, chopped
2 garlic cloves, finely minced
3 or 4 ripe plum tomatoes
 skinned and chopped

1/2 teaspoon dried oregano
1/2 teaspoon dried marjoram
1/2 teaspoon thyme
3 *chipotle* peppers (in *adobo* sauce), finely minced
3 tablespoons adobo sauce from *chipotles*
Salt to taste
1/4 cup chopped cilantro

To serve:

1 dozen *tostadas* or whole corn tortillas, fried crisp

1/2 small head lettuce, shredded

2 small avocados, cut into thin slices

Lime wedges

Cover the pork with water and cook with the garlic and bay leaves until the meat is tender, about 35 minutes. Set aside to cool. When the meat has cooled, remove from liquid and shred meat, reserving the meat liquid. Remove chorizo from casing and cook in skillet until lightly browned. Drain chorizo on paper towels. Pour off fat from skillet, except for about 2 tablespoons. Add the chopped onion and minced garlic to the skillet and cook for about 3 minutes. Add tomatoes, oregano, marjoram, and thyme. Simmer on low for about 5 minutes until the juice has cooked out of the tomatoes. Add the *chipotles* and

(continued)

adobo sauce and mix well. Add the shredded pork and drained chorizo. Add about 1 cup of the meat cooking liquid and bring to a boil. Turn heat to low and let simmer for 15 minutes, adding liquid as needed. Let most of the liquid cook away. Stir in half of the chopped cilantro, reserving the remaining cilantro for garnish. Season to taste with salt.

To serve, place about 3 tablespoons of the *tinga* on a crisp corn tortilla. Cover with shredded lettuce, top with avocado slices, and sprinkle a little of the chopped cilantro on top. Serve with lime wedges.

Note: This dish can be more stew-like by increasing the liquid slightly. If served this way, it is usually eaten rolled in warm flour tortillas.

Puerco a la Naranja con Camote – Pork in Orange Sauce with Sweet Potatoes

1 cup white vinegar
1 teaspoon *achiote* paste
1 teaspoon ground cumin
2 cloves garlic, finely minced
1 teaspoon salt
1/2 teaspoon black pepper
2 pounds lean boneless pork, cut into 1-inch cubes

2 tablespoons olive oil
2 cups water
1 cup fresh orange juice
1/3 cup lemon juice
2 sweet potatoes, boiled and peeled, sliced 1/4-inch thick
1 sliced orange, for garnish

In a large bowl, combine vinegar, *achiote* paste, cumin, garlic, salt, and pepper, stirring to mix. Drop in pork cubes, turning so they are coated in the mixture. Cover the bowl and refrigerate for at least 6 hours or overnight.

Remove pork cubes from marinade, reserving liquid. Pat meat cubes with paper towels to remove moisture. Heat oil in heavy skillet over high heat and add pork cubes and fry until golden brown. Drain off fat from pan. Add the reserved marinade and water, and bring to boil over high heat, scraping loose any brown bits clinging to side and bottom of pan. Reduce heat to low, cover and simmer pork for about 45 minutes or until tender. Stir in orange juice and lemon juice and simmer for about 5 minutes. To serve, arrange hot sweet potato slices on platter and pour pork cubes and sauce over them. Garnish with fresh orange slices.

Lomo en Salsa de Membrillo – Pork Tenderloin in Quince Sauce

The Spanish brought the quince tree to Mexico where it was well suited to the warm climate, and quinces were soon incorporated into Mexican cuisine. The quince is related to pears and apples. A fruit paste called "ate" is made of quince and is a popular sweet in Mexico.

1 (2 to 2-1/2-pound) pork tenderloin
2 cloves garlic, sliced
1 teaspoon cinnamon
1/2 teaspoon nutmeg
Salt and pepper to taste

1 onion, sliced
2 cups white wine
4 quinces, peeled, cored, and cubed
1/2 cup water (divided use)
2 fresh jalapeños, top removed, finely minced

(continued)

Make small incisions in the meat and stud it with garlic slices. Sprinkle meat with cinnamon, nutmeg, salt, and pepper. Place meat in small roasting pan with the sliced onions and wine. Cover and bake in 375° oven for 1 hour. While the meat is cooking, place the quince cubes in saucepan with 1/4 cup water and cook until soft. Place quince in blender or food processor and purée until smooth. Add the minced jalapeños to the purée mixture. Pour the quince sauce over the meat and bake uncovered for 40 more minutes, basting often. Remove from oven and let stand 5 minutes before serving. Place meat in serving dish and pour quince sauce over meat.

Note: If you cannot find fresh quince, you can substitute unripe pears, which will be a little sweeter than the quince.

Costillas de Cerdo a la Crema – Creamed Pork Chops

This recipe comes from central Mexico and uses parsley, a favorite seasoning in Mexico. Serve with Mexican squash (calabazas) *and white rice* (arroz blanco).

6 pork chops
2 tablespoons oil
1/2 onion, finely chopped
1/2 cup chopped parsley

1 cup sour cream
1/2 cup water
1 tablespoon mustard
Salt

Fry the pork chops in oil, turning until well cooked and browned on both sides. Remove chops from pan to platter and keep warm in 150° oven. Remove any excess oil or fat from pan. Gently fry the onion and parsley in skillet until limp. Add sour cream, water, and mustard and simmer on low for 2 minutes. Add salt and pepper to taste. Pour sauce over chops. Serves 6.

Carnitas – Crispy Pork

Here is a popular way to fix pork in Mexico. This dish can be used for making tortas, gorditas, *and tacos.*

3 pounds pork, shoulder, or butt roast	1 teaspoon oregano
2 cloves garlic	Salt and pepper
1 onion, chopped	Water to cover
	2 tablespoons oil

Place all ingredients in heavy cooking pan and bring to boil. Cover and simmer on low until meat is tender, about 2 hours. Allow meat to cool in liquid. Remove meat from liquid and shred meat with fork.

Heat 2 tablespoons oil in heavy skillet and cook meat until it is browned and crisp.

Mariscos – Seafood

Bernal Díaz del Castillo, the Spanish warrior who recorded the landing of Cortez's men at Veracruz and their trek to Mexico City in 1519, marveled at the abundance of fresh seafood. He told how over 300 runners relayed the freshly-caught fish from the coast to Montezuma's palace so the emperor could have fresh seafood on his table each day.

This same king also sent runners to the snow-capped mountains to gather ice. The ice was served with sweetened fruit juices and was considered to be the supreme dessert.

Camarones Borrachos – Drunken Shrimp

2 pounds large raw shrimp (24-30 shrimp), peeled and veins removed

Marinade:

1 tablespoon olive oil
4 tablespoons lime juice
1 teaspoon salt
1/2 teaspoon pepper
4 or 5 cloves garlic, finely minced
2 tablespoons Worcestershire sauce

1 teaspoon Mexican oregano
2 fresh jalapeño peppers, seeds and stems removed
1/2 cup finely minced cilantro, stems removed
1/3 cup tequila
2 tablespoons butter

Mix marinade ingredients except butter and pour over shrimp, mixing well to coat shrimp. Cover and refrigerate for 1 hour. Heat a large skillet until very hot. Add shrimp and marinade. Cook 2 to 3 minutes until shrimp turn pink and are cooked through. Remove shrimp to serving dish and add 2 tablespoons butter to skillet to thicken sauce. Cook briefly and pour sauce over the shrimp.

Mariachi – Music

Wearing broad sombreros, band members play joyful and romantic music representing the heart and soul of Mexico. Legends say this music originated in Jalisco from the Coca Indians living in and near Cocula. Others say the name mariachi comes from the French word "marriages" and the custom of having musical groups at weddings. Some attribute the name mariachi to the state of Nayarit and the Pinutl language. Guadalajara, Jalisco is considered the mariachi capitol of the world and has an annual celebration with musicians from Mexico and around the world.

Ceviche – Pickled Fish

The acid in the fresh lime juice "cooks" the fish. Ceviche *is a popular dish in most Latin American countries. In Peru, it is served with popcorn.*

1 pound pompano, haddock, or sea
    bass fillets
Salt and pepper to taste
2 or 3 ripe Roma tomatoes
1 tablespoon rice wine vinegar
1/2 teaspoon oregano

Juice of 6 or 7 limes
4 pickled jalapeño chiles,
    chopped
4 tablespoons olive oil
1 small onion, sliced
2 avocados

Wash the fish fillets, remove any skin, and cut into small pieces. Place in a glass dish and pour lime juice over all. Let stand in refrigerator for 3 to 4 hours, turning fish pieces with a wooden spoon from time to time. A half hour before serving, dice the tomatoes and add to the fish. Mix the olive oil, vinegar, oregano, salt, and pepper. Pour over fish and add pickled chiles. Serve ice cold in sherbet glasses or shells garnished with slices of the onion and avocado. Have tortilla chips or crackers on the side.

Feria Nacional de la Plata – **National Silver Fair**

Taxco, Guerrero is the site of silver mining and exporting. In November, silver-smiths compete against craftsmen from around the world. There is a festival including concerts, dancing, and fireworks. Unusual silver items are offered for sale.

Huachinango a la Veracruzana – Red Snapper Veracruz-Style

Veracruz has long been famous for its seafood. Mexicans traditionally make a pilgrimage to this city to eat the freshly-caught fish. This dish is the most famous served in Veracruz with good reason. The whole fish, covered in red tomato salsa topped with green olives, is a special-occasion dish. Next time you are lucky enough to have a 4 to 5 pound snapper, try this recipe.

1 whole (4 to 5-pound) red snapper   2 limes

Place fish in glass baking dish and prick skin with fork. Squeeze lime juice over fish, place the lime shells into the cavity of the fish, and let stand for 3 hours. Remove lime shells and sprinkle fish with salt and pepper. Preheat oven to 375°.

Sauce ingredients:

2 tablespoons oil
1 onion, coarsely chopped
2 cloves garlic, finely minced
4 ripe tomatoes, peeled and chopped
2 tablespoons capers, drained
20 stuffed green olives

3 jalapeño peppers, stemmed,
 seeded and finely chopped
1/2 teaspoon oregano
1 bay leaf
Salt and pepper to taste
Lime slices, for garnish

Heat oil in heavy skillet; add onion and garlic. Cook until onions are clear. Add remaining ingredients except lime slices, and cook for 10 minutes.

Pour sauce over the fish and bake uncovered in 375° oven for 30 minutes. Carefully turn fish over and bake another 25 minutes or until fish flakes easily. Serve with rice and lime slices. Serves 6 to 8.

Camarones Adobados – Shrimp in *Adobo* Sauce

1-1/2 pounds large shrimp (about 24), shelled and de-veined

***Adobo* Sauce:**

4 large *ancho* chiles	1/4 cup olive oil
3 to 4 tablespoons warm water	1/2 cup white wine
1 medium onion, chopped	1/4 cup white vinegar
2 garlic cloves, minced	1/2 teaspoon sugar
1/4 teaspoon oregano	1/2 teaspoon salt

Remove stems, seeds, and de-vein chiles. Tear chiles into small pieces. Place in bowl with 1-1/2 cups hot water and soak for 30 minutes. Drain the chiles, reserving the water. Place chiles in blender or food processor. Add onion, garlic, and oregano along with 3 to 4 tablespoons of the soaking water, and purée until smooth. Heat oil in heavy skillet over moderate heat. Add the chile purée and cook, stirring constantly about 5 minutes. Add wine, vinegar, sugar, and salt; simmer on low for 5 minutes, stirring constantly.

Add shrimp, stirring to coat. Cover and simmer on low until shrimp are cooked through, about 4 to 6 minutes. Season with salt and serve over rice. Makes 4 to 6 servings.

Mexican Riddle

Fui a la plaza	I went to the plaza
Compre de ella.	To buy her.
Vine a mi casa	I come to my house
Y llore con ella	and cry with her.
Advina lo que soy	Guess what I am?
La cebolla.	The onion.

Pescado en Salsa de Chile – Fish in Garlic Chile Sauce

2 pounds whitefish fillets
1/3 cup flour
1 teaspoon crushed chile pequin
1 teaspoon salt
1/3 cup oil

1/3 cup butter
8 cloves garlic, finely minced
1/4 cup lemon juice
1 tablespoon chopped parsley

Combine flour, chile, and salt. Coat fish fillets with mixture. Heat oil in skillet. Sauté fish for 3 to 4 minutes per side over medium heat. Remove to warm platter.

Melt butter in saucepan, sauté garlic until lightly browned. Add lemon juice and parsley. Cook over low heat until bubbles form. Pour over fish fillets. Run fillets under broiler for 1 minute. Makes 6 to 8 servings.

Postres – Desserts

Prior to the Spanish invasion of Mexico, fresh fruits, often sweetened with honey, were eaten with a meal. The most famous Mexican food of all, chocolate, was mixed with water and served as a bitter drink. Chocolate is important in desserts.

The Spanish introduced dairy cattle to Mexico, which resulted in new foods such as milk, butter, and cheese. Catholic nuns used these dairy products to make traditional Spanish milk-rich desserts, which quickly became popular with the native population.

Flan Clásico – Classic Flan

The flan, a milk and egg custard, is Mexico's most popular dessert. It is easy to see why: the perfect ending to a spicy meal with its creamy texture and caramel syrup coating. This recipe makes a sweet dense flan that is sure to be a favorite. Use boiling water to fill the pan and add more boiling water as needed while the flan cooks.

1 cup sugar
4 eggs
1-1/4 cups milk

1 (11-ounce) can sweetened
  condensed milk
2 teaspoons vanilla

Place sugar in skillet and cook on moderate heat, stirring until sugar is melted and a golden brown color. Do not allow to burn or scorch. Remove from heat and cool slightly, then pour into a 1-quart baking dish. Swirl the sugar mixture around to coat sides and bottom evenly. Beat eggs until light. Add milk, condensed milk, and vanilla. Stir until well-blended. Turn into prepared baking dish. Place dish in pan of hot water (about 1-inch deep). Bake at 325° for 1 hour and 30 minutes, or until a knife inserted in center comes out clean. Let cool thoroughly, then turn out on serving plate. The flan can be made ahead and refrigerated until serving. Makes 6 to 8 servings.

Flan de Chocolate – Mexican Chocolate Flan

This recipe takes the Mexican flavors of chocolate and cinnamon and combines them in the traditional dessert, the flan.

1/2 cup sugar	1 cup milk
2 tablespoons water	1/4 teaspoon cinnamon
Juice of 1 lemon	2 whole eggs
2 ounces semi-sweet chocolate	2 egg yolks
	4 tablespoons sugar

Combine the first amount of sugar with the water and lemon juice in a small heavy skillet. Cook over low heat until the sugar dissolves. Swirl the pan from time to time, but do not stir. Once the sugar liquifies, bring the syrup to a boil and cook until golden brown.

While preparing the syrup, heat 4 individual custard cups in a 350° oven. When syrup is ready, pour into heated custard cups and swirl to coat the sides and base evenly. Leave to cool at room temperature.

Chop chocolate into small pieces and heat with milk and cinnamon, stirring occasionally to help the chocolate dissolve. Whisk the whole eggs and yolks together with remaining sugar until slightly frothy. Gradually whisk in chocolate milk mixture.

Carefully pour chocolate custard into the custard cups and place them in a baking pan. Pour hot water in pan to a depth of 1 inch. Place the pan in 350° oven and bake custards until just slightly wobbly in the center, about 20 to 25 minutes. Cool at room temperature, then refrigerate for several hours or overnight before serving. Loosen custards carefully from the sides of dishes, using a thin knife, and invert onto serving plates. Shake to allow the custard to drop out. Makes 4 servings.

Crepas de Cajeta – Caramel Crepes

Cajeta *is caramelized goats' milk, sweet and rich, almost a candy. The name* cajeta *means little box. In Mexico,* cajeta *was once sold as a confection in small wooden boxes about 4 or 5 inches wide. Now you can find it in jars in the Mexican food section of many supermarkets. This recipe makes a special-occasion dessert. The crepes can be made ahead and the dessert assembled just before serving.*

12 dessert crepes
1/2 cup chopped, toasted pecans

Sweetened whipped cream*
1 jar *cajeta***
Fresh strawberries for garnish

Crepas:

1-1/4 cups flour	2 cups milk
1/2 teaspoon baking powder	2 eggs
2 tablespoons sugar	2 tablespoons melted butter
1/2 teaspoon salt	1/2 teaspoon vanilla

Mix flour, baking powder, sugar, and salt. Stir in milk, eggs, melted butter, and vanilla. Mix or whisk until thoroughly blended. Let batter rest in refrigerator for 1 hour. Heat an 8-inch skillet and drop in about a tablespoon of butter which should melt instantly. Pour 1/4 cup batter into the skillet and quickly rotate the pan so the batter covers the bottom in a thin layer. Return to heat and cook until light and brown. Loosen with a wide spatula, turn and cook on the other side. When brown, place crepe on plate covered with waxed paper. Keep adding

(continued)

butter and making crepes until all the batter is used. The crepes can be made ahead and kept covered.

To toast pecans, spread on cookie sheet and bake in 350° oven about 15 minutes. *Whip cream, add powdered sugar; flavor with Mexican vanilla, or use purchased whipped topping. Slice strawberries, slightly crushed with sugar; make about one hour ahead.

Place *cajeta* in bowl and add a little milk to thin. Cook in microwave on medium low, stirring once or twice until mixture is warm and thinned, adding more milk as needed.

To assemble dessert

Spread about 1 tablespoon of the *cajeta* on a crepe, sprinkle with some toasted pecans and roll up into a tube. Repeat with remaining crepes. Reheat in low oven, about 250°, a few minutes before serving. Place 2 crepes on each plate, spoon on whipped cream, and top with sliced strawberries. Makes 6 servings.

**Making *Cajeta*

If you cannot find *cajeta*, you can make your own with a can of sweetened condensed milk.

Remove label from can and place unopened can in a heavy saucepan and cover with water. Cook over low heat for about 2 hours. With tongs turn can over and cook for 2 more hours. Be sure can stays covered with water. You can also cook the *cajeta* in a slow cooker for the same amount of time. Cook and refrigerate overnight before using. If *cajeta* is too thick, thin with milk or a little brandy.

Pastel de 15 Años – Fifteenth Birthday Cake

In Mexico, when a girl reaches a fifteenth birthday, her family holds a celebration called a *Quinceañera*. It is like a sweet sixteen party and debutante's coming-out-ball all rolled into one, announcing to the world that the girl has left childhood behind and is now a woman. The girl is dressed in a beautiful white or pastel floor-length ball gown with a matching head dress and bouquet. A religious ceremony is held first, followed by an elaborate dinner and dance. One of the most important food dishes for the *Quinceañera* is the birthday cake. Some families, if finances permit, order a tiered cake as elaborate as a wedding cake from the local *panadería* (bakery). The icing on the cake is usually tinted to match the girl's *Quinceañera* dress. Here is a recipe for a traditional homemade version of the *Pastel de 15 Años*.

10 eggs, room temperature
1 cup sugar
1-2/3 cups cake flour

1 teaspoon baking powder
1/4 teaspoon salt
1 (12-ounce) jar pineapple or
    apricot preserves

Preheat oven to 350°. Grease and flour two 9-inch cake pans. Separate eggs, placing whites in large bowl. In separate bowl, beat egg yolks and sugar until sugar is dissolved and mixture is light and creamy. Sift flour, baking powder, and salt together and gradually add to beaten egg mixture. In the large bowl, beat the egg whites until stiff peaks form; add vanilla. Gradually fold the egg-flour mixture into the beaten egg whites. Place batter in 2 pans and bake for 25 minutes or until toothpick inserted in the center comes out clean. Remove from oven and let cool in pans 5 minutes, then turn out on rack to cool. Once completely cooled, slice each cake in half horizontally to make four layers.

(continued)

Place one layer on plate, spread top with more preserves; then place second cake on top. Repeat with rest of layers. Spread tops and sides with icing. Decorate cake with candles, coconut, or colored sugar, and place flowers around the edge of plate.

Frosting:

2 cups granulated sugar
1/8 teaspoon cream of tartar
1 cup water

1 teaspoon vanilla
1-1/2 to 2 cups powdered sugar

In a medium saucepan, combine sugar, cream of tartar, and water. Cook over medium high heat, and bring to boil without stirring, until mixture reaches thin syrup stage (226° on candy thermometer). Cool slightly, then stir in vanilla and powdered sugar; stir until icing is thick and will not drip off the spoon. Frost cake while icing is still warm.

Buñuelos – Fried Christmas Cookies

This sweet confection is served during the Christmas season after each evening's posadas. *It is usually served with cinnamon tea or hot chocolate. Starting in late November, you can purchase large hand-made cookie cutters shaped like flowers, stars, bells, and crosses in the local hardware stores. The cutters are used to make the Christmas* buñuelos.

1 cup anise tea, prepared

4 cups flour

1/2 teaspoon salt

2 tablespoons sugar

1/4 cup lard or shortening

1 egg, beaten

Oil for frying

Cinnamon-sugar for sprinkle

Prepare anise tea by boiling 3 teaspoons anise in 1 cup water. Set aside to cool.

(continued)

Sift dry ingredients and cut in lard or shortening using a pastry cutter. Add beaten egg and anise tea, mixing well. Turn dough out onto greased board and knead for five minutes. Place dough into refrigerator for one hour. Roll dough out on floured board to a 1/4-inch thickness. Cut into shapes with cookie cutter and prick with fork so they will puff. Fry cookies in hot fat until golden brown. Drain on paper towels and sprinkle lightly with a mixture of cinnamon and sugar. Makes 4 to 6 dozen cookies.

Día de la Candelaria – Candelmas Day

This national holiday on February 2, notes the end of Christmas celebrations. Tamales and atole (a hot sweet drink thickened with corn flour) are enjoyed. In Tlacotalpan, Veracruz, a port city, a bull is rafted into town and released.

Bebidas – Beverages

In Mexico, fresh fruit drinks are favorites sold on street corners and in restaurants. The taste of sweet fruit drinks goes well with the spicy local dishes. Mexicans also like herbal drinks; many times they are consumed for their medicinal qualities. And who can forget the most famous drinks of Mexico using chocolate or tequila? In pre-colonial times, chocolate was a drink reserved for royalty, the wealthy, and warrior classes. It was served as a bitter drink, flavored with chiles and herbs. Chocolate beans were a major crop for the Mayans and they traded them with other tribes. The cocoa bean was even used as a currency in the early Aztec marketplaces. The Europeans mixed chocolate with milk and sugar.

(continued)

The beverage crossed the ocean back to Mexico where native cooks added cinnamon and whipped the drink with a wooden beater called a *molinillo* to create a head of foam on top. Mexican chocolate is sold in packages of round tablets with other Mexican foods. The tablets consist of chocolate, spices and sugar ready to add to liquid. Chocolate is a favorite breakfast drink usually accompanied by pan dulce (sweet rolls).

In addition to limeade, limeade mixed with mango nectar, and lemonade, Mexicans enjoy watermelon pulp mixed with water and sugar as well as cantalope processed in a blender with added water and sugar to taste. An aromatic tea is made by boiling 2 tablespoons of anise seed, steeping 15 to 20 minutes, straining, adding 3 tablespoons of sugar to dissolve. The most famous Mexican liquor is tequila, which is from the sap of the agave, a plant related to the lily.

The hearts of these plants, eight feet tall and twelve feet in diameter, are tapped for sap. Prior to the Spanish invasion, the sap was allowed to ferment into a drink called *pulque*.

The Spaniards taught the people how to distill the agave sap into the clear liquid we call tequila. The traditional way of drinking tequila involves three ingredients: lime, salt, and tequila. First sprinkle a little salt on the knuckle of your hand, hold the lime slice between your thumb and forefinger, take a suck of the lime, then a lick of the salt and a drink of tequila. The frozen Margarita, which is said to have originated near Tijuana in the late 1940s, is the most popular drink served in Mexican restaurants in the United States.

There is an annual fair featuring tequila producers giving demonstrations. Held at Tequil, Jalisco, there are rodeo events, cock fights, mariachi bands and fireworks.

Classic Margarita

Juice of 1/2 lime
1/2 ounce of Triple Sec
1 ounce tequila

Combine the ingredients in a mixing glass with cracked ice. Shake and strain into a chilled margarita or champagne glass that has been edged in salt. To edge in salt, run the rim of the glass with a piece of lime, then dip and turn in a saucer of salt.

A frozen Margarita has 1-1/2 ounces tequila, 1 ounce lime juice, 1/2 ounce Triple Sec and 1 teaspoon sugar (optional). Combine ingredients in a blender with 1/2 cup cracked ice and blend until slush. Garnish salted glass with a piece of lime.

List of Recipes

Mexican Saying
Dime con quién andas y te diré quién eres.
Tell me who you go with
and I'll tell you who you are.

BOOKS BY MAIL

Penfield Stocking Stuffers have approximately
160 to 170 pages. You may mix titles. Books retail for $6.95 each or postpaid:
1 for $10.95; 2 for $18; 3 for $25; 4 for $30; 6 for $45; 12 for $80
Complete catalog of all titles $2.50 Prices and availability subject to change.

Recipes from Old Mexico (this book)
License to Cook New Mexico Style
License to Cook Texas Style
License to Cook Arizona Style
Tales of Texas Tables
Texas Cookoff

Penfield Books
215 Brown Street
Iowa City, Iowa 52245-5801
Tel (800)-728-9998
Fax (319)-351-6846
Email penfield@penfieldbooks.com
www.penfieldbooks.com

El Castillo – The Pyramid

El Castillo at Chichén Itzá (as seen on the back cover) was recently voted one of the seven new wonders of the world. The 78-foot-tall pyramid has 91 steps on each of its four sides. The total number of steps plus the top platform equals 365, signifying the calendar year. The pyramid site measures solar phenomena throughout the seasons. During the equinox the shade of the steps projected on the guardrails appears like a snake coming down the stairs. At the end of the equinox, the snake recedes back. Ancient observatory ruins are found nearby. This was an important site for the Mayan astronomical system and was dedicated to the god Kukulcan (also named Quetzacoatl). The Mayan culture dates back 3,000 years and was deemed a highly developed civilization. The temple and city of Chichén Itzá was abandoned in A.D. 1400 prior to the Spanish invasion.